TANZANIA IN AFRICA

Published by:

AFRICAN PUBLISHING GROUP (INTERNATIONAL)
E-mail: apg@africaonline.co.zw
PO Box BW 350, Harare
Zimbabwe

First published 2004

ISBN: 1-77916-046-1

Edited by: Phyllis Johnson
Readers: Inyasi Lejora and Dr Alan Rodgers
Design: Tonely Ngwenya, Harare
Printing: DS Print Media, Johannesburg

CONTENTS

ACKNOWLEDGEMENTS

I am particularly grateful to the Director General of Tanzania National Parks (TANAPA), Gerald Bigurube, his predecessor Lota Melamari and Inyasi Lejora, the TANAPA manager for Ecological Monitoring, for their support during this important project.

African Publishing Group International has published 15 full-colour, area-specific books on Tanzania in its Into Africa Travel Guide series. These cover: Serengeti, Olduvai/Laetoli, Ngorongoro, Lake Manyara, Tarangire, Arusha (town, park and Mount Meru), Kilimanjaro, Saadani/Bagamoyo, Zanzibar, Mafia Marine Park and Kilwa, Mikumi, Udzungwa, Ruaha, the Selous Game Reserve and Lake Victoria (including Rubondo Island National Park). And there are still more to come!

These guide books are pocket-sized and user-friendly. They vary from 64 to 96 pages in length (except Zanzibar that is 160 pages), and obviously contain more information about individual parks and other tourist attractions than is possible in this single overview.

This book gives readers a taste of all of Tanzania's parks and other tourist attractions as well as beginning to give Tanzania as a whole its well merited and separate, long-overdue tourist destination identity.

In the course of completing this volume and the 15 area-specific guide books referred to above, I have met and interviewed scores of people in the government, TANAPA, the Wildlife Division, Ngorongoro Conservation Area Authority, Zanzibar, at the facilities where I have stayed, guides, charter and travel operators, and others connected with the tourism industry. They are too numerous to thank individually.

But two people I must single out for particular mention are my main reader in Tanzania, Dr Alan Rodgers, who has read and commented on all of the Tanzanian books in manuscript form. I have accepted most of his comments and have endeavoured to make the necessary changes.

The final word is reserved for my wife, Phyllis Johnson, who accompanied me on some of these Tanzanian journeys and who has been the series editor. Without her support and encouragement the area-specific guide books and this volume would not have seen the light of day.

David Martin
Tanzania
2004

INTRODUCTION

Frequently I am asked by prospective visitors to Africa: "Where should I go on my first safari?" Unhesitatingly I answer: TANZANIA.

Then the would-be visitor asks: "And which national park or other attraction should I visit?" Without avoiding their question my reply is equally unhesitating: "Visit all of them. They each have their own character and characteristics."

Each of mainland Tanzania's 14 national parks and Jozani on Zanzibar fit into a particular niche and while I have my favourites in the north, coast/east, south and west, it is only by sampling each that the visitor will determine which are their favourites.

Tanzanian statistics

United Republic of Tanzania is the country's full name
The country is 945,166 sq km (364,943 sq miles) in size
The population of Tanzania is estimated at 32 million
Swahili is the official national language
English is widely spoken, particularly at tourist resorts
The official currency is the Tanzania shilling
Tanganyika was a British trusteeship from 1919
Independence of Tanganyika was on 9 December 1961
Zanzibar was a British colony from 1890
Independence of Zanzibar was on 10 December 1963
On 12 January 1964 the majority took over from the Omanis
This African uprising was known as the Zanzibar Revolution
On 26 April 1964, the two countries united as Tanzania
Multi-party elections are held every five years
Black, yellow, green and blue are the colours of the flag
Dodoma in central Tanzania is the political capital
Dar es Salaam on the coast is the commercial capital
Giraffes are protected and are the national animals
Kilimanjaro, Serengeti and Ngorongoro are in Tanzania.

Opposite page: The stately giraffe is Tanzania's national animal that may not be hunted.

Male lion resting

Nyerere before Tanzania's 1961 independence

Getting to Tanzania is now relatively easy. There are direct flights from Europe to Dar es Salaam, Kilimanjaro and Zanzibar as well as from a number of neighbouring countries, Ethiopia and South Africa. This is backed up by a good internal air system as well as by tarred roads. Scores of tour operators, curio shops and good restaurants exist.

Awaiting the visitor is the warm embrace of the Tanzanian people. Most countries and travel agents claim that the people of a given country are the most friendly in the world. As one who has lived and travelled extensively in Africa for over 40 years, I can report first-hand that the Tanzanian people are the friendliest I have encountered anywhere.

Tanzanians are proud of their country, their sovereignty, their first president, *Mwalimu* (Swahili for teacher) Julius Nyerere, and the peaceful way in which they have passed his mantle to his successors. Even after his death they revere his words and are guided by his principles.

Nyerere is remembered primarily for two things: his contribution morally and materially to the liberation of southern Africa and for the way in which he moulded his nation.

In April 1994 when South Africa attained majority rule, Nyerere's and Tanzania's dream was partially realized. For almost 50 years, he had been the main spokesperson opposing white minority rule in the three Portuguese colonies of Angola, Guinea Bissau and Mozambique, and in Southern Rhodesia, Namibia and South Africa. Often he drew the opprobrium of some of the western countries.

But liberating a nation, as Nyerere realized, was one thing; building it another. At home he made Swahili the national language thereby binding the 125 ethnic groups with a single identity, created a Tanzanian ethic, and preached and practiced simplicity.

He was a man of principle, a rarity among contemporary politicians anywhere in the world, and he was readily predictable. He had offered to delay his country's independence to coincide with that of Kenya and Uganda so the three could create a federation. Thus, although for different reasons, the 1964 union with Zanzibar came as no surprise.

Young Tanzanian girl

Impalas drink   Stately gerenuk poses

Tanzania leads the world

Over 28 percent of Tanzania's almost 1 million sq km is set aside as national parks, conservation areas, game and forest reserves, and as game controlled areas. This total includes the Selous Game Reserve that is larger than Switzerland.

There are 14 national parks on mainland Tanzania plus 31 game reserves, Ngorongoro conservation area, 5 forest reserves, 2 biosphere reserves and 4 UNESCO World Heritage Sites.

The list also includes the country's marine parks and reserves, the Selous-Niassa corridor linking the wildlife populations of Mozambique and Tanzania and new game reserves uniting the two countries along the Ruvuma River in the hitherto "forgotten" south of Tanzania.

No other country in Africa or the world can boast such a unique policy of nature conservation and wildlife protection at a national level and it is an ironic comment that while Tanzanians may be economically among the poorest people, they are potentially the richest on the planet in terms of biodiversity.

Elephants

Nyerere's legacy lives on in the minds and actions of Tanzanians, who were amazed at his state funeral in October 1999 to find diverse foreign dignitaries heaping praises upon him. Suddenly Tanzanians recognized that Nyerere was an international figure as well as their own icon.

A million Tanzanians from across the country attended his funeral when he was laid to rest beside his parents in Butiama village close to Lake Victoria. They remembered the good things he had done for his country, for southern Africa and for the world beyond.

While in normal conversations Tanzanians may sound noisy, they are little afflicted by the bombast and arrogance that touches some other parts of the continent and the world.

They are, in my view, a genuinely warm and hospitable people whose use of the word *karibu* (meaning "welcome" in Swahili), is genuinely offered to outsiders, no matter their colour or creed.

Tanzania was once regarded as the Cinderella country of East Africa, and this may be a blessing in disguise. While the northern neighbour Kenya temporarily prospered, Tanzania was left behind. Now the sleeping giant is vigorously stirring and the number of tourists visiting Tanzania has already overtaken the total for Kenya.

Tanzania's best-known park internationally is the Serengeti, declared in 1951. But the 14,763 sq km Serengeti National Park, despite being larger than Northern Ireland and containing some 2 million wild animals, has a bed-capacity of only 790. Entry fees into the park for visitors are US$30 per day and because the bed-limit is strictly implemented, visitors are spared the sight of zebra-striped mini buses around every lion, the Serengeti having some 2,500 of this species.

The Selous Game Reserve in Tanzania has the largest population of African hunting dogs that are left in the wild.

But peace, the people, and the lessons learned are not the only reasons to visit a country. Beyond that it must have specific attractions that serve as the real lure for the visitor. And in this, among sub-Saharan countries, Tanzania is without a rival.

Mount Kilimanjaro, the Serengeti, Ngorongoro Crater and Zanzibar are all in the United Republic of Tanzania. So too is Olduvai Gorge, hailed as the birthplace of humans, the Selous Game Reserve, more parks and reserves than any other country, and innumerable historical monuments.

These parks and reserves contain the greatest concentrations of wild animals found anywhere in the world. There are an astounding 1.5 million wildebeests and over 250,000 zebras as well as a similar number of Grant's and Thomson's gazelles on the Serengeti plains alone.

Added to the truly amazing spectacle of the annual migration of wildebeest and zebra are lion, leopard, cheetah, hyena, warthog, jackal, bat-eared fox, elephant, buffalo, giraffe, hartebeest, topi, mongoose and a host of other species that are relatively common.

Olduvai Gorge is on the Serengeti's eastern plains and physically in Ngorongoro Conservation Area. The site is strangely eerie as befits its ancient status. Here in 1959, Mary Leakey uncovered the skull of *Zinjanthropus* or the "Nutcracker Man" as the media dubbed it on account of its enlarged back molars.

Louis and Mary Leakey devoted 60 years of their lives to Olduvai Gorge in their search for the origins of our early forebears. There they were to find the jaw of *Homo habilis*, nicknamed the "Toolmaker", and *Homo erectus*, a direct descendent of ours.

Twenty-five km to the southwest, Mary later found 3.6 million-year-old footprints of three hominids walking across the landscape. The "Laetoli Trackway" as it is known, contains the earliest footprints left by our ancestors. Olduvai/Laetoli truly contains the "book of life" as stated by a German butterfly collector after visiting the site in 1911.

Tanzania, of course, is millions of years older than such "modern" finds. A German mining engineer, Bernhard Sattler, prospecting for garnets and other precious minerals in 1907, found his way blocked by huge fossil bones protruding from the ground. He had accidentally stumbled on the massive Tendaguru dinosaur graveyard.

The Laetoli footprints

The Brachysaurus dinosaur from Tendaguru in the Berlin Museum

The remains of the vast *Brachysaurus* dinosaur that confronts the visitor to the Berlin Museum of National History came from Tendaguru. It was transported bone by bone overland and meticulously reassembled in Germany.

Louis Leakey had begun his Tanzanian career in 1924 at Tendaguru, a little known and somewhat inaccessible attraction in the southeast of the country inland from the port of Lindi.

He was part of a British expeditionary force that had to find their own dinosaurs, two of which from Tendaguru are now in British museums.

Near Iringa town, close to Ruaha National Park, are the important Stone Age sites at Isimila. Dramatic sandstone columns stand as mute sentinels and some of the tools and weapons found at the site have been dated as being over 60,000 years old.

To the north near Lake Manyara National Park, is Engaruka. The outlines of a series of stone huts and irrigated fields are all that remain of the site 80 km north of the village of Mto wa Mbu (Mosquito Creek in Swahili), that the visitor must pass through before climbing the towering Gregory Rift Wall on the way to Ngorongoro and Serengeti.

The occupants of Engaruka left the site 500 years ago, their identity and reasons for leaving still shrouded in mystery. At Kondoa and elsewhere in Tanzania there is plentiful rock art, while at Kilwa there are the ruins of the once prosperous city-state that traded with the east more than 700 years ago.

Group of seven black rhinoceros photographed at Ngorongoro

Ngorongoro Crater has its own majesty and is the largest extinct volcano in the world. Here the visitor finds the most easily seen group of black rhinoceros in Tanzania, as well as innumerable other species ranging from five prides of lions to wildebeest and zebra. And the Lerai forest has the most heavily tusked elephants you are likely to see anywhere.

Looking down from the rim of Ngorongoro at the crater (it is correctly a caldera formed by the volcano sliding into itself) one is stunned by the beauty 200 metres below and the fact that two German brothers once farmed the 261 square km crater.

To the east is another extinct volcano, Kilimanjaro. Rising 5,895 metres (19,650 feet) from the Maasai Steppes, this snow-capped peak is Africa's highest mountain. Less than 150 years ago, supposed geographical experts in Europe questioned the existence of snow so close to the equator.

Since then it has become an inspiration for successive generations of black nationalists in Africa, a lure for climbers from around the world, and the name for the book, *The Snows of Kilimanjaro*, by the American writer, Ernest Hemingway.

The islands of Zanzibar, once fiercely contested by Arabs and Europeans, have their own special allure. Approached from the sea, the House of Wonders dominates the main island's skyline. Inland, particularly on Pemba, are the cloves for which the islands are famous.

Picking cloves in Zanzibar   *Stone Town house of Tippu Tip*

Narrow streets mark the ancient Stone Town of Zanzibar, with cars, motorbikes and bicycles whizzing around corners. Scattered throughout Zanzibar there is plentiful history, including the remnants of Portugal's 200-year occupation of the Indian Ocean, the former slave market, the houses of infamous slavers such as Tippu Tip, and David Livingtone's house.

Zanzibar, and much of the coastal mainland, has pristine white sand beaches. Beyond them is the Indian Ocean containing innumerable species of very colourful fish and coral, and Tanzania so far has two marine parks and several marine reserves.

The Selous Game Reserve measures almost 50,000 sq km and is the largest wetland reserve on the continent set aside for the preservation of wildlife. Despite the poaching scourges of the 1980s, the Selous still contains at least 65,000 elephants, the largest concentration in the world.

Trenches and spent bullet cases remain from the First World War when the military commander of German East Africa, Paul von Lettow Vorbeck, made the longest strategic guerrilla retreat in modern warfare thereby keeping hundreds of thousands of Allied troops from the European theatre for over three years.

In between all of these highlights are a myriad of other attractions. On the southern circuit are Mikumi and Ruaha with vast herds of elephants, and the little known Udzungwa Mountains National Park that is ideal for hikers and which has the largest altitudinal range of closed forest.

To the west is Katavi National Park with its vast herds of buffalo and pods of hippopotamus, and the Mahale and Gombe national parks that are the habitat for chimpanzees. They border on Lake Tanganyika, Africa's deepest lake.

Lilac-breasted roller

To the northeast is Lake Victoria, a vast shallow lake that British explorer, John Hanning Speke, found was the source of the River Nile. Located only a few km from the western gate of the Serengeti, this lake also contains Rubondo Island National Park.

This 69,000 sq km lake (26,000 square miles) is second in size only to Lake Superior on the Canada-US border and contains an amazing one million tonnes of fish, the fillets of Nile perch being ferried in giant transport planes to Europe and elsewhere.

Tanzanite

It is said that Tanzanite was "discovered" in the window of a jewellery shop in New York. According to the story, a curious Tanzanian diplomat saw a stone that sounded like his country in the window of Tiffany's .

Upon enquiring within, he was told that the stone came from 40 km (25 miles) southeast of Arusha. The jeweller had popularised the stone giving it the name "Tanzanite".

Since those days in the 1960s, the demand for Tanzanite has increased dramatically. The stone comes only from Tanzania and lilac-blue coloured stones are the most valuable.

To Mwanza's east lies Lake Manyara, a gathering point for vast flocks of flamingo and other waterbirds, Tarangire with the largest number of elephants in northern Tanzania, and Arusha, the safari capital, with Mount Meru, Africa's fourth highest mountain, towering over the town. Nearby are the Tanzanite mines, one of Tanzania's many mineral deposits.

Pair of dikdik

On the coast is Saadani, soon to be Tanzania's first coastal national park, north of Bagamoyo, the old slaving and ivory entrepot. Near Mbeya in the Southern Highlands is the Kitulo Plateau, a mountain grass area notable for its wild orchids and other flowers.

Tanzania has 1,119 identified birds, innumerable colourful butterflies, at least 30 species of antelopes and many types of insects, indigenous flowers and trees. This is more than exists in any other East African country.

Gaudy commodore butterflies change colours with the seasons.

Having visited almost all of these Tanzanian tourist highlights in the past 40 years, I thought that I knew something about them. How wrong I was. It was only when researching, writing and photographing area-specific guidebooks to Tanzania that I began to truly learn more about these places.

With the wisdom of hindsight, I now realize that producing the area-specific guide books before embarking on this book of Tanzania's national parks or on other definitive guides to Tanzania, was a necessary preparatory process.

I hope that you will feel the same passion for Tanzania that I do at the end of your African safari. In the meantime, as Tanzanians say, *safari njema* meaning in Swahili, "have a good journey".

David Martin
African Publishing Group
Tanzania, 2004

ARUSHA NATIONAL PARK

This little gem of a national park near Arusha, northern Tanzania's safari capital, is a perfect way to begin or end an African safari. It contains species that the visitor will not see elsewhere in northern Tanzania, its environment is unique and it is on your doorstep.

Much of this 137 sq km park combines an audible forest experience with a visual one. Birdcalls, black-and-white colobus monkeys crashing through the trees and a host of other sounds are drowned out by a vehicle's engine. So switch it off, remain silent and hear the calls of the wild.

Brief profile

Located only 35 km from Arusha town
Officially declared a national park in 1960
Giraffe, buffalo and elephant are common
Black-and-white colobus monkeys live here
There are no lions but there are leopards
Kilimanjaro two-horned chameleons may be seen
More than 575 species of birds identified
A diverse habitat for tropical butterflies.

Situated on the eastern edge of the Great Rift Valley, this unique park contains volcanic Momella Lakes, Ngurdoto Crater and Mount Meru, the fourth highest peak in Africa.

At 4,565-metres (15,064 feet), Mount Meru towers over the nearby Arusha town, and is topped in Africa only by Mounts Kilimanjaro, Kenya and Rwenzori, all in East Africa.

Mount Meru is a sombre mountain known to the local Maasai people as *Ol Doinyo Orok*, meaning the "black mountain". In contrast, the Maasai call snowcapped Kilimanjaro, lying 80 km to the east, *Ol Doinyo Oibor*, meaning the "white mountain".

The moods of Mount Meru vary wildly. In the winter months, snow briefly dusts the summit while for the remainder of the year it is sunbathed. Once it was a volcano, but the fires that fuelled it are now extinct, the last minor eruption occurred in 1877.

The crater wall of Mount Meru was ruptured by a series of explosions 250,000 years ago. The eastern wall of the crater was blown away, sending lava, mud, rocks and water cascading across the Sanya Plains almost as far as the town of Moshi in the foothills of Kilimanjaro.

Opposite page: Black-and-white colobus monkey

Momella Lakes in the northeast of Arusha National Park were formed in the depressions of the drying mud. Today these lakes are noted for the varied bird life that inhabits the shallow freshwater and saline lakes.

Ngurdoto Crater is also an extinct former volcano. Molten rocks, possibly from two cones, withdrew towards the earth's centre creating Ngurdoto which, like Ngorongoro, is a caldera created by the inward collapse of a volcano.

The crater is on the right after the entrance gate and the road around it forks soon after with Leopard Hill road on the left that can be slippery in the wet season. But, conditions and transport permitting, it is well worth a visit.

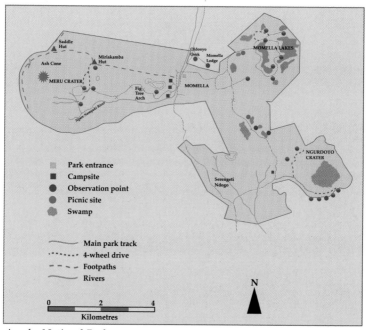

Arusha National Park

Leopard Hill road leads to two viewing points, Leitong at 1,853 metres (6,115 feet) being the highest point. The crater below is 3 km across and comprises of forest and swamp interspersed with open plains.

People are not allowed into the crater, but you will see well-defined trails made by animals ascending and descending. Elephants, herds of buffalo, giraffes and warthogs are all visible to the naked eye. Ngurdoto is a reserve within a reserve. Binoculars will bring it all closer.

Tracing the route back, the visitor will encounter the pink flowering "touch-me-not" that literally explodes when touched. After the start of the light rains, scarlet and globular fireball lilies are seen in shady damp places from December to February.

Fireball lily

Climbers from throughout the world come to conquer Mount Meru and the nearby Mount Kilimanjaro. Mount Meru's lower, inhabited slopes rise gently from the park gate to 2,100 metres (6,930 feet) at Miriakamba Hut and you can drive this section.

Mount Meru at dawn

Three days should be allowed for the ascent and descent of Mount Meru; a sleeping bag, warm clothes and your own food are necessary, and armed and trained parks guides are compulsory in case dangerous animals are encountered.

After Miriakamba, the ascent becomes steeper. The trail from here first heads north before turning west to Saddle Hut. The cliff between the summit and Ash Cone is over 1,500 metres (4,950 feet) in height and is one of the tallest cliffs in the world.

On its face you may see klipspringers, rough-coated antelope the size of goats that leap from one rock to another on narrow, cylindrical hooves. Lammergeier vultures may soar overhead, dropping bones to break on the rocks below so that they can extract the marrow.

From the summit, as well as much of the way to it, the views are spectacular. Kilimanjaro, dwarfing all other mountains in Africa, rears from the Maasai Steppes and to the west is the Great Rift Valley. At the visitor's feet is the national park containing Ngurdoto Crater and Momella Lakes.

Climbers at the summit of Mount Meru

Ngurdoto and Meru are among the few places on earth where you can appreciate the beauty and tranquillity of dry montane forests. This is home to many species of birds, some of which are more often heard than seen.

Climate

The lighter, short rains should fall in November and December. This is followed by a lull before the long rains from March until mid-May.

Depending upon altitude, the rains can vary from up to 800 mm (32 inches) to 1,700 mm (68 inches) per annum. During the cooler months from June to September, heavy morning cloud helps to keep the grass green.

The hottest months are January and February when the temperature can rise to 27 degrees C. In the cold season from late June until August the temperature drops to 15 degrees C. Warm clothing is needed during this period.

Flock of silvery-cheeked hornbills roost just before dawn on the Rift (left) and Great white pelican (right)

The Silvery-cheeked hornbill is a noisy resident in the canopy, and its raucous braying call echoes through the forest. The spectacular purple Hartlaub's turaco with its bright red underwings makes a somewhat softer but equally raucous call.

Tropical boubou are black and white, and tend to skulk in the vegetation. Their bell-like duets are commonly heard near viewpoints around Ngurdoto Crater. Crowned eagles, Forest and Auger buzzards may also be seen.

The brilliant green and red Bar-tailed trogon is among the rare birds in this habitat. It measures 24 cm and spends most of the short forays from its perch in the shadows snatching insects from the air.

The countryside around Momella Lakes is undulating, with generally treeless hills and open grassland. The lakes are fed by underground streams and are very shallow and alkaline. Their alkalinity attracts many waterbirds including pelicans, flamingos, cormorants, geese, grebes, ibises and storks.

Many waterbirds that use these wetlands are migratory species and therefore the European winter months that coincide with the African wet season months from October to April are the best time to visit.

Because of their varied mineral content, each lake supports a different type of algal growth and has a different colour. One of the lakes, separated by a narrow strip of land, contains quite fresh water in which hippopotamus reside.

Drivers should note that the rules dictate that they must drive anti-clockwise around the lakes. Hippopotamus can be seen near the island on Small Momella Lake while buffalo, bushbuck, waterbuck and Bohor reedbuck graze in the early morning and late evening.

One of the most outstanding features of Arusha National Park is the bewildering array of butterflies.

Mother of Pearl butterflies (left) may be found near the main Ngurdoto gate to the park while Christmas butterflies (right) are found in many places throughout Tanzania.

There are about 18,000 butterflies worldwide, over 20 percent of them in Africa. Tanzania, with some 1,400 species, has the highest number in east Africa and it was a butterfly collector who first saw the potential at Olduvai Gorge.

The vegetation lining the road towards Momella Gate is mainly *Dodonaea viscose*. This small tree or shrub is extremely hardy, withstanding fires and often becoming the secondary growth where the original forest has been felled. It is not eaten by the wild animals and has thin leaves and yellow-green flowers.

One small animal frequently seen in this area is the banded mongoose. It is a stocky animal with a wiry coat marked by dark traverse bands. They live in groups of up to 30 and will often be seen following elephant or buffalo trails, continuously twittering as they search for dung beetles and millipedes.

Mongoose on a termite mound

A traditionally dressed Maasai with his red blanket and stick hurrying past a woman, modern in dress but undertaking a familiar female chore

The significant agricultural settlements bordering on the park are a stark reminder of just how vulnerable protected game areas such as this one are to encroaching human occupation.

Located midway between the Cape and Cairo, Arusha town is where most visitors stay and it is perfectly placed for a visit to the national park. This is one of Tanzania's most fertile areas; bananas and coffee are the main crops of the Warusha and Wameru people.

Only a century ago, Arusha was described as "an oasis in the wilderness". Today modern cars and handcarts compete for space on the roads, vendors clutter the pavements, and hotels and restaurants cater for all tastes and budgets.

KILIMANJARO

Snow-capped Mount Kilimanjaro in Tanzania just south of the equator is the highest point of Africa and one of the highest freestanding mountains in the world, rising to 5,895 metres (19,340 feet) above sea level. It dwarfs any mountain in America or Europe and has inspired hope among generations of Africans as a symbol of freedom and independence from colonialism.

In the days before global warming, Kilimanjaro had considerably more glaciers and snow than is the case today and it was this barrier that confronted early climbers. Now scientists believe that the last Kilimanjaro glacier will be gone by 2025.

Brief profile

Mount Kilimanjaro comprises three extinct dormant volcanoes
These are Kibo, the highest at 5,895 metres (19,340 feet)
Mawenzi 5,140 m (16,992 feet) and Shira 3,962 m (13,075 feet)
Kilimanjaro ranks twelfth in the world in height
Mount Everest, the highest, is 8,848 m (29,028 feet)
Kilimanjaro rises 4,800 m (15,840 feet) from the plains below
At its widest, it is 40 km (25 miles) across.

Geologically, Kilimanjaro's origins are traced back to the Great Rift Valley which reached its present form between one and two million years ago, a relatively recent development. Originally, where Kilimanjaro stands today, there was a gentle undulating plain and a few old eroded mountains.

About a million years ago, the plain buckled and slumped. Fractures and faults allowed the molten lava below the earth's crust to reach the surface. Volcanoes emerged along the Great Rift Valley and the plains became a patchwork of volcanic cones and craters.

There followed the birth of Kilimanjaro some 750,000 years ago, as it literally pushed its way upward from the fractures in the earth's crust.

Opposite page: Campers at 4,000 metres in the Karanja Valley on their way to the summit

The earliest human history of Kilimanjaro remains obscured in the mysteries of time. Given the mountain's fertile environment, it is reasonable to suppose that our ancestors gathered food and hunted animals on the lower slopes long before written records existed.

The first known written reference was some 18 centuries ago, when Ptolemy of Alexandria, an astronomer and the founder of scientific cartography, wrote of an unknown place he called Rhapta. Certainly Rhapta was south of Somalia. Inland of Rhapta, Ptolemy said, there existed a great snow-capped mountain. This was surely what we now call Mount Kilimanjaro.

Another (usually ignored) reference occurred in the 13th century, when an Arab geographer, Abu'l Fida, spoke of a mountain that was white in colour.

Kilimanjaro's icefields are captivating and intimidating.

During the 19th century, Kilimanjaro became a stopover and provisioning point for trade caravans of porters and slaves from the interior, and in May 1848, Johann Rebmann, a Swiss-German missionary, was shown the mountain by a respected African caravan leader, *Bwana* Kheri.

Rebmann, reputed to be the first European to see the snow-capped mountain, wrote in his diary: "I observed something remarkably white on top of a high mountain and first supposed it was a very white cloud."

Climbers skirting the Rebmann glacier at 5,700 metres (18,810 feet)

When Rebmann wrote in the *Church Missionary Intelligencer* the following year, about what he had seen with his own eyes, the armchair geographers in Europe rebuked him. Britain's geographer said Rebmann was imagining things, as there could not be a snow-capped mountain just 330 km (206 miles) south of the equator.

Elephants instead of towns

It now seems inconceivable that little more than 150 years ago the very existence of snow on Mount Kilimanjaro was disputed in Europe. The satirical English poet, Jonathan Swift, poking fun at the geographers, wrote:

*"So geographers in Afric maps
With savage pictures fill their gaps
And o'er uninhabitable downs
Place elephants instead of towns."*

It was not until 5 October 1889 that Kilimanjaro was finally conquered by Dr Hans Meyer, a German whose country was Tanganyika's first colonizer. Maybe Africans had scaled the mountain before, but there is no record of this. Meyer's achievement is today commemorated with a bronze plaque that bears a photograph of him.

Since then Mount Kilimanjaro has been conquered by thousands of others, including a motorcyclist who rode to the summit from where others have hang-glided. American journalist and adventurer, Ernest Hemingway immortalized the mountain in his book, *The Snows of Kilimanjaro*.

Exhausted climber lies down at the summit.

East African colonial history books once taught pupils that Kilimanjaro was given as a gift by Britain's Queen Victoria to her grandson, Wilhelm (the German Kaiser), because he did not have a snow-capped mountain in his empire.

Kilimanjaro

It's a good romantic story, but it is not true, although Kilimanjaro was part of a colonial exchange: the port of Mombasa was given to British-ruled Kenya, while Dar es Salaam and Kilimanjaro were given to German-ruled, colonial Tanganyika.

Kibo became known as Uhuru (Freedom) peak after Tanganyika's independence from Britain on 9 December 1961, when a young army officer planted the national flag at the summit.

The people who live on the mountain today are the WaChagga. They have been there for at least 400 years although where exactly they came from is in doubt. Possibly they came from the north. Some oral traditions, however, suggest they originated from the mountain, were "dropped" onto it, came from the plains, or from the east or the west.

The WaChagga are probably a hybrid fusion of many ethic backgrounds or, as it has been put, "a cross-breed grouping". They are to be found running businesses in almost every corner of Tanzania.

On the lower slopes of Kilimanjaro, they grow bananas and cultivate coffee, legacies of *Mangi* Sina, recalled as one of the five dominant leaders in Chagga history. He ruled in the difficult period of the transition from militarism to diplomacy, thereby keeping the German colonizers at bay.

Candle of Hope

"We, the people of Tanganyika, would like to light a candle and put it on top of Mount Kilimanjaro which would shine beyond our borders giving hope where there was despair, love where there was hate, and dignity where before there was only humiliation," said Julius Nyerere on 22 October 1959, addressing the Tanganyika Legislative Assembly.

Nyerere's "Candle on Kilimanjaro" speech inspired generations of African leaders and the mountain became the symbol of liberation from colonialism for Tanzanian and southern African nationalists.

Picking coffee (left) and banana flower (right)

Today it is recognized that the main attraction is Kilimanjaro itself and the desire to conquer it, although it has a small national park by the same name.

The peaks that rise starkly from the plains below are visible from the Arusha-Moshi road and from Kilimanjaro International Airport.

Some 20,000 people a year scale the mountain to Uhuru and Mawenzi peaks. Over 80 percent of them trek up the mountain by the easier "Coca Cola" or Marangu route. The more seasoned go by the tougher "whisky" routes.

To climb the mountain, visitors must provide details of their planned route and schedule in case mountain rescue becomes necessary. They must use authorized guides, and it is advisable to take porters.

Kilimanjaro can be very cold, particularly near the summit. Visitors need to kit themselves out properly with walking boots, warm clothing, gloves, sunglasses and a balaclava.

The beautiful Impatiens kilimanjari do not occur anywhere else

Altitude sickness is not uncommon and is exhibited in the form of chronic headaches and vomiting. Nevertheless, the number of people scaling Kilimanjaro has doubled in the past decade and an 87-year-old man and a 6-year old boy have made it to the summit.

The Marangu route is clearly marked all the way to the summit. This route takes about five days and the following times between huts, is only a rough guideline. The initial climb to Mandara Hut from the park entrance takes about 4 hours, to Horombo Hut 5 to 7 hours and to Kibo Hut 5 hours.

Everlasting flower (left) and Lobelias, relative of the common garden plants

Next comes the climb from Kibo Hut to the summit and then down to Horombo Hut. This climb usually starts around 2 am (or earlier) when the scree (small stones) is frozen, with the climber viewing the sunrise over Mawenzi peak and getting back to Horombo Hut.

On the final day, the climber descends to Mandara Hut for lunch, and then heads back to the park gate at Marangu. There are several other routes such as those from Mweka, Umbwe, Machame and Shira. For advice on these it is necessary to consult the Kilimanjaro Mountain Club or Tanzania National Parks (TANAPA).

During the climb the visitor will pass through five distinct ecological zones that are governed by altitude, rainfall and temperature that in turn dictate plant and animal life.

The lower slopes are densely populated up to 1,800 metres (5,940 feet) and in the wetter east the rainfall can be 1,800 mm (72 inches) per annum. Livestock and cultivation have changed the face of this area from the former bush, shrub and lowland forest that once existed.

In the forest zone, from 1,800 metres to 2,800 metres (9,240 feet), rainfall is high on southern and eastern slopes (1,500 mm or 60 inches a year). On the northern and western slopes the rainfall is about half.

This is Kilimanjaro's most fertile coffee zone where about 90 percent of Kilimanjaro's water originates. Montane forest embraces the mountain and the rainfall percolates through the thick carpet of leaves, soil and porous lava rock to emerge into springs below.

In the heath and moorland zone up to 4,000 metres (13,200 feet), the rainfall and the temperature drop, and

Porcupine

frost and sunshine are ever present. The peaks, although still distant, become visible and after Mandara Hut, giant heather begins.

The highland desert begins at 4,000 metres and continues to 5,000 metres (16,500 feet). Rainfall is only 250 mm (10 inches) per annum and the seasons meet in this zone; summer by day and winter by night. The almost lunar landscape minimizes the number of plants, mammals, birds and insects.

The summit is even barer. Here you encounter typically Arctic conditions: sub-zero temperatures at night and blistering sunshine by day. Oxygen is about half the amount at sea level, there is virtually no surface water, and little to protect you from the sun's rays.

LAKE MANYARA NATIONAL PARK

Looking down from the western Rift wall along the road to Ngorongoro and the Serengeti, it is easy to see why Lake Manyara National Park was once described as "the emerald of Africa".

The lake shimmers below in the heat haze, home to flamingos, pelicans and innumerable other water birds. Between the lake and the Rift, the park, with one main road and several loops, stands out in luscious greens that contrast with the arid, brown and windswept countryside.

Brief profile

Lake Manyara National Park was declared in 1960
During British rule it was an important hunting area
The park is 330 sq km in size; two-thirds of this total is lake
Two extensions to the western end of the park have been made
One of these, a dry season elephant refuge, was added in 2002
A distinctive feature of the park is the groundwater forest
This includes tall trees, intermediate shrubs, grasses and plants.

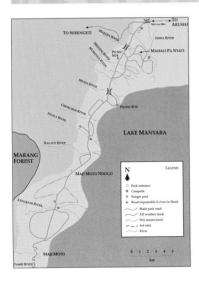

The land part of the park is long and thin. The boundaries at the eastern end where the visitor enters the park, and at its western end, are narrow. The single main road through the park is virtually hidden in the trees at the foot of the escarpment.

But as the visitor gets closer, the green mass seen from the rift wall takes on an individual identity. There are two types of palm trees, several acacias, mahogany, croton, false mvule, sweetberry, quinine, sycamore, fever, baobab and a host of other trees, bushes and shrubs.

Opposite page: Manyara is famous for its tree-climbing lions.

Just on the left of the main entrance gate to Lake Manyara National Park, a wispy, succulent *Euphorbia tirucalli* grows in a square patch of manicured green lawn. It is from this shrub-like plant, called *Mtupa mwitu* in Swahili, that Manyara derives its name.

In Maa, the language of the Maasai, *"emanyara"* means a kraal where these nomadic travellers stockade their livestock at night away from wild animals and human poachers. To build the stockade they use *Euphorbia tirucalli,* called *Ol oile* in Maa.

Geological forces spanning millions of years moulded the area, creating the Mbulu Plateau between Manyara and Ngorongoro, and extending from what is now the Sudan/Ethiopia border in the north to Mozambique in the south.

Central to this was the upheaval that created this part of the Great Rift Valley some 12 to 15 million years ago during what geologists call the mid-Miocene epoch.

Eventually stretching over 10,000 km (6,500 miles) from Turkey in the north down to the mouth of the Zambezi river in Mozambique, the Rift is a fault in the earth's crust which now dominates much of eastern Africa.

Lake Manyara National Park, described as "the emerald of Africa", with the lake behind and the wall of the Rift Valley on the right.

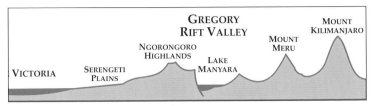

Block diagram of region showing Lake Manyara

The section of the Rift at Manyara is named after Scottish geologist, John Walter Gregory who coined the phrase "rift valley" to describe the stark geology he saw when he surveyed it towards the end of the 19th century.

Mount Kilimanjaro, Mount Meru, and Ngorongoro were formed later by this volcanic activity. All are now dormant although Oldoinyo Lengai (Maasai for the Mountain of God), 50 km north of Manyara near the Kenyan border, had a smoke and ash eruption in 1966.

The settlement of Mto wa Mbu on the edge of Manyara is well watered and fertile, situated near a fast-flowing river. The water feeding this and the ground forest in the park emanates from Ngorongoro.

The rich agricultural land and related business opportunities have attracted immigrants from all over Tanzania.

The creation of Mto wa Mbu as a centre for agriculture, commerce and tourism led to the displacement of the pastoral Maasai. Today many Maasai live on the more open and arid plains or around Ngorongoro Crater. To the far south are the Barbaig people.

Tanzania's only active volcano, Oldoinyo Lengai, last erupted in 1966.

The Iraqw people who live between Manyara and Ngorongoro are agriculturalists, growing cereals and beans, and maintaining limited livestock. In contrast, the Barbaig and Maasai are pastoralists moving with their cattle in search of grazing and water. Their main foods of meat, milk and blood come from their livestock.

Manyara's groundwater forest begins just inside the main gate. This has some of the characteristics of a lush green, tropical rain forest with shafts of sunlight cutting through the heavy foliage and the sounds of birds and mammals echoing through the trees.

Two types of palms

The groundwater forest has a high water table that is fed by seepage from the volcanic rocks of the Rift wall, in contrast to a tropical rain forest which is watered by direct and heavy rainfall.

Lake Manyara National Park is renowned for its tree-climbing lions (although lions climb trees in other parks). Why they do so is not known. The most likely explanation is that they climb into the branches to get away from the unwelcome attention of flies and large mammals that may threaten them.

The park is also notable for its elephants and is reputed to have the highest density of these animals of any park in the world. Zebra, wildebeest, buffalo and giraffe can be seen in the open areas near the lake, impala and waterbuck in forest glades, and klipspringer on the rocks near the western end of Manyara.

Waterbuck (left) and Klipspringer (right)

Baboons and vervet monkeys are also common. Just inside the gate or on the Rift Wall the visitor may encounter troops of baboons, while vervet monkeys are found along the road and around picnic sites. These and other wild animals should not be fed by people as this only encourages them and can be dangerous.

What really sets Lake Manyara apart is its bird life, particularly the concentration of water birds. Many species of flamingo, pelican, geese, duck, teal, stilt, stint, avocet, heron, egret, stork, spoonbill, ibis, thicknee, plover, fish eagle, hamerkop and hornbill are among the more than 380 identified birds.

The occurrence of volcanic lava and ash (rich in sodium and phosphate) is common throughout the region and accounts for the high alkalinity at Manyara. Due to dry season evaporation and the closed system of Lake Manyara, this alkalinity results in the formation of soda crystals in the lake which attract flamingos, pelicans and innumerable other water birds.

Glossy ibis in the centre surrounded by White-faced ducks

Lesser flamingo can be distinguished from Greater flamingo by their smaller body size, very dark red beak and more crimson coloured feathers. Ninety percent of flamingo seen in East Africa are Lesser. They feed on blue-green algae while Greater flamingo feed on small shrimps, their differing diets thus allowing co-habitation.

Identifying Pink-backed from Great white pelicans is more difficult. The Great white is physically larger, but it does have a pinkish tinge to its feathers. They are strong fliers, frequently rising on the thermals well above the Rift Wall.

Spur-winged geese are the largest African waterfowl, distinguished by their long necks, legs and black-and-white plumage. They exist in pairs or small flocks and are very wary.

Egyptian geese are the most vocal of the species and they will perch on anything, including a sleeping hippopotamus. They are buff-brown with a chestnut eye patch and they swim with their rear ends held high.

Climate

Lake Manyara National Park receives 760 mm (30 inches) of rain a year and if it was not for the seepage from the rift (originating in the Ngorongoro highlands), the park's groundwater forest would not survive.

The rainy season at Manyara should start in November and, with a brief lull in January/February, continue until May. The heavy rains in March/April may temporarily restrict mobility. The area is also subject to droughts.

Knob-billed geese have black-and-white dappled feathering and the male is easily recognizable by the large, fleshy, black comb at the base of his beak.

Among the teal are the Hottentot and Red-billed, while ducks include Fulvous whistling, White-faced whistling and Yellow-billed.

Elegant Black-winged stilts are common along the rift but Manyara is one of the few places in Tanzania where the Avocet breed.

Lake Manyara National Park has accommodation for all budgets. It has a total bed-capacity of 803 with campsites, *bandas* (self-contained huts of local construction), a hostel, three economy campsites, a number of guest houses in Mto wa Mbu, and a more upmarket hotel and lodges on the Rift where most visitors stay.

Goliath heron, Africa's largest heron

NGORONGORO CRATER

From the viewing point hundreds of metres above Ngorongoro Crater, the panorama spreads out in a vast amphitheatre. The hills rise smoothly from the crater floor through evergreen forest, and rain clouds cascade over the eastern rim.

Viewed from above, it seems as if you have polished Aladdin's magic lamp and wished. But this is not the world of make-believe and as the visitor drives down the descent road, the black dots below become discernable shapes, with the crater becoming ever more beautiful and irresistible.

Brief profile

Ngorongoro Crater Conservation Area is the name of the area
It is 8,292 sq km, varying in altitude from 1,020 to 3,587 metres
The crater is 19.2 km in diameter and 610 metres deep
It is 261 sq km, contains a soda lake and abounds with wildlife
The terrain of NCCA embraces many different habitats
These include mountain forest, highland heath and bushland
As well as dry grassland, swamp and Acacia woodland
Rainfall in the Ngorongoro Highlands supplies Lake Manyara
Most rain falls on the eastern and southern slopes
Olduvai and the Serengeti side are in the "rain shadow".

Zebra and wildebeest mix on the crater floor along with some 50 lions, 400 spotted hyenas, Grant's and Thomson's gazelles, various types of jackal, Greater and Lesser flamingo and many other species. In all, Ngorongoro has some 25,000 animals, making this the most intensive game-viewing area on earth.

Certain species, such as giraffe, do not enter the crater. Herds of buffalo are seasonal while in Lerai forest only male elephants are found, the females preferring not to descend the crater walls when pregnant or accompanied by their young.

Opposite page: Black rhinoceros at Ngorongoro

Flowers such as *Aloe secundiflora, Crinum macowanii* (pyjama lillies) and *Abutilon mauritianum* decorate the descent road. Halfway down on the right is *Euphorbia candelabrum*, a large candelabra tree that looks like a cactus but is not, and near the bottom are colonies of the untidy grass nests of Rufous-tailed weavers which are found only in northern Tanzania.

Pyjama lilies

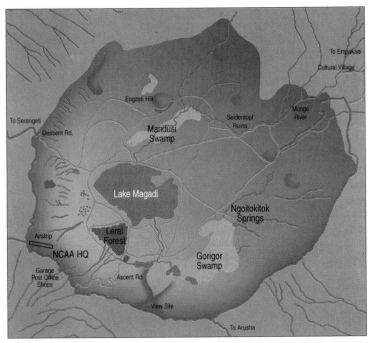

Ngorongoro Crater

Ngorongoro Crater is more correctly a caldera. This is caused by the inward collapse of a volcano with the caldera being many times the size of the original vent through which it once emitted lava and gas. Ngorongoro Crater is the world's largest unflooded and unbroken caldera. It is 19.2 km in diameter and 604 metres deep. The whole Ngorongoro conservation area, including the crater, is 8,292 sq km in size and altitudes within it vary from 1,020 to 3,587 metres.

The crater was once part of a chain of seven volcanoes that spewed their ash over the surrounding countryside. Now only one of the volcanoes 40 km away, remains active -- Oldoinyo Lengai which means The Mountain of God in Maa, the Maasai language.

Climate

The moisture-bearing clouds from the Indian Ocean to the east are broken up by the high ground they encounter. The short rains tend to come from the northeast while the long rains come from the southeast.

Clouds tumbling over Ngorongoro's eastern face at dawn.

As the rain clouds make their way from the sea, they lose some of their moisture before reaching Ngorongoro. Once there, much of the rain falls on the eastern and southern slopes nurturing the rain forest and providing the catchment for the Mbulu District.

The western (Serengeti) side of Ngorongoro receives comparatively little rainfall and is technically described as being in the "rain shadow". On the way down towards Serengeti, the landscape changes dramatically with Commiphora shrub and scattered Acacia trees.

Ngorongoro lies in the Rift Valley that stretches through much of Africa from the Red Sea in the Middle East. The split in the super-continent Pangaea some 200 million years ago began the process of shifting the landmasses to their present locations.

Africa took its present position some 70 million years ago, and this long period of geological upheaval resulted in the creation of the 6,500 km long African or Great Rift Valley some 15 to 20 million years ago.

The area in its present form is 2 to 3 million years old. Ngorongoro volcano, at its peak 4,587 metres (15,137 feet), collapsed inward while the nearby highlands were subjected to a momentous upheaval with a large circular fracture developing around Ngorongoro.

Basins were created that became lakes such as Eyasi, Manyara and Natron, and calderas such as those at Empakaii and Olmoti. The lakes are alkaline as there is no outflow and they attract large numbers of flamingoes at various times of the year.

Some 50,000 Maasai people live in the conservation area where they were resettled and promised permanent rights to land and water, but since the 1970s they are forbidden from living in the crater itself.

Maasai in crater with livestock

Today, Ngorongoro is defined as a multiple usage area where the indigenous people, the visitors and the wildlife are protected. But, perhaps inevitably, the emphasis has been on the visitors and the wildlife, although it is now recognized that the wildlife can only survive with the cooperation of the indigenous people.

Just how important livestock are for the nomadic Maasai is illustrated by the usual greeting when two Maasai meet: *"Keserian ingera? Keserian ingishu?"* ("How is your family? How are your cattle?" in the Maa language).

On the way from Ngorongoro to Serengeti, visitors may see donkeys and cattle grazing with zebra around Maasai *manyattas* (houses) in the Malanja Depression on their left. The stockades around the houses, to keep the animals in at night (and human poachers and wildlife carnivores out), are made from *Euphorbia tirucalli*.

Four different factors determine the life of wild animals – food, security, shade and water. In that they are little different to humans although the people can make some of their own whereas the wildlife have to live within their habitat.

Animals need shade from the mid-day sun. Thus the morning and evening game drives are most profitable for visitors, as they will see the animals grazing. Most animals drink regularly at the cooler times of the day when many species can often be seen close to water.

Heavily tusked Lerai elephant

Insofar as security is concerned, zebra, wildebeest, Grant's and Thomson's gazelle graze on the open plains keeping an ever-watchful vigil for predators. Elephants dislike lions that may prey on their young, and even tiny banded mongoose leave at least one of their number on sentry duty to keep watch for predatory birds.

In the wild, almost every animal watches for another species. Leopards carry their prey up trees to avoid the unwelcome attention of hyenas and lions. Cheetahs fear hyenas that can break their backs with a single bite of powerful jaws. A decade ago, no cheetahs were found in the crater, although they can now be seen there.

Side-striped, black-backed and golden jackals as well as spotted hyenas are likely to be found close to wildebeest and gazelle. Eland, Africa's largest antelope with it spiral horns, are found around Lerai forest near the ascent road, while hippopotamus are most commonly seen submerged in the Mandusi Swamp.

Defassa waterbuck also live in the fringes of the Lerai groundwater forest while the diminutive and shy Bohor reedbuck may be seen around Gorigor Swamp. In all, 115 species of animals have been recorded in the conservation area and of these 50 were located on the crater floor.

The cover and terrain also determines the birds, butterflies and reptiles that inhabit an area. Some species of birds are seedeaters usually found in the grasslands. Others eat fruit and prefer the forest habitat. Yet another category is for waterbirds.

Crowned crane (left) and Saddle-billed storks

A flock of Greater flamingos feeding at Ngorongoro's Lake Magadi

Everything you will see on your safari has a reason for being where it is and has carved out its own particular niche. The habitat dictates the resident species and in this the rains are the key factor.

It now seems extraordinary that two German brothers named Seidentopf farmed the whole of Ngorongoro crater before the First World War, and that the remains of their houses and a plough still mark their passing.

After Germany's defeat in the First World War, Tanganyika become a British Trust Territory and German property was seized. The country gained independence in 1961, and three years later, after the union with Zanzibar, was renamed Tanzania.

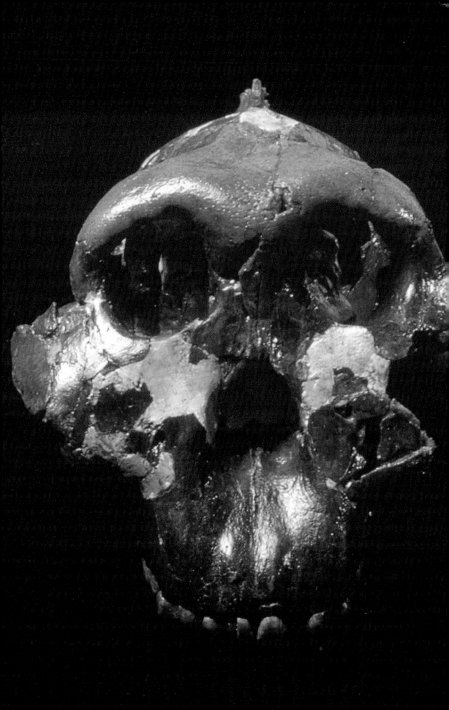

OLDUVAI/LAETOLI

In front of the main viewing platform at Olduvai Gorge is "The Castle", a distinctive and weather-moulded gigantic mound that contains some clues to the historical secrets that encompass this part of northern Tanzania.

"The Castle"

Layers of volcanic ash lie heaped on top of each other giving the mound different colours and making the task of archaeologists somewhat easier as they seek to unravel the mysteries of our past in this now arid and barren region where once there was a lake.

The museum behind Olduvai's viewing platform provides some further clues as to the secrets. The prehistoric tools and the bones of extinct animals, and the exhibits, tell their own story of yesteryear.

The Acheulean handaxe

The Acheulean hand axes found at Olduvai, usually made from large lava flakes, are some 1.4 million years old. The Acheulean culture, that probably ended in Africa some 200,000 years ago, is also found in Europe and parts of Asia. It is probably the longest and most widespread of all pre-historic tool-making traditions.

Opposite page: Reassembled skull of Zinjanthropus found by Mary Leakey in 1959 at Olduvai, nicknamed "Nutcracker Man" due to large back molars.

Olduvai Gorge with "The Castle" in the foreground and the mountains beyond

The first European known to have seen Olduvai Gorge was a German butterfly collector, Professor Wilhelm Kattwinkle. In his notes in 1911, he described Olduvai as containing "the book of life" and he took back to Berlin a considerable number of fossils including the teeth of an extinct three-toed horse known as *Hipparion*.

Kattwinkle's finds came at the end of the "golden age" of scientific exploration although other Germans followed, notably Dr Hans Reck who was supported financially by the German Kaiser.

About 1.7 million years ago, and continuing intermittently ever since, Rift Valley faulting has cut Olduvai Gorge in a number of places. Reck numbered the 50-km-long gorge's faults from one to five and this gradation is still used.

Climate

Olduvai is hot and dry with the wind blowing from the east for much of the year. Average rainfall is 57 mm per annum, mainly between December and May. Temperatures range from 12 degrees C at night to 33 degrees C at noon in the shade.

You will notice the changing landscape as you drop down the western side of Ngorongoro towards Olduvai. Now you are in the "rain shadow" with Maasai homesteads (*manyattas* in Maa), domestic stock and wildlife intermixed.

The grass turns from green in the wet season to golden brown and *Acacia* and *Commiphora* scrub dot the landscape. Broken strands of woodland dominated by flat-crowned *Acacia* mark the shallow valleys and the few watercourses that feed Olduvai.

The gorge runs from west to east with two shallow lakes, Ndutu and Masek, at the southern head. Once a prehistoric lake covered Olduvai and the area is very rich in fossils and the living sites of early people.

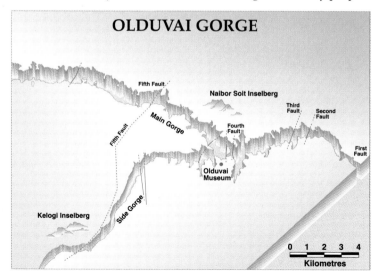

Mary Leakey working on the Laetoli footprints

Twenty-five miles to the southwest of Olduvai are the 3.6-million-year-old Laetoli footprints, the earliest our forebears are known to have left, a replica of which is featured in the museum at Olduvai.

These show three people, an adult male and female and a child, walked across the landscape leaving their footprints for posterity. Coming in from one side are the hoofprints of *Hipparion*, an extinct three-toed horse, and a foal.

These evocative Laetoli footprints are important for several reasons. In the first place, they are the oldest known footprints in the world.

Second, they prove that as early people gradually evolved from apes into humans, they stood up on their hind legs so that their arms were free to direct missiles and other weapons at wild animals and perceived human enemies.

Third, although they were made 3.6 million years apart, the Laetoli footprints and those made on the moon on 21 July 1969 by American astronaut, Neil Armstrong, are the most famous in the world.

Laetoli footprint and Armstrong's on the moon

The "Laetoli Trackway", as it is known, was a recent find in 1978, and it was discovered accidentally. Late one evening, three conservationists were making their way back to camp after an archaeological dig. As they walked they played, throwing large balls of dried elephant dung at each other.

Dropping to his knees under the hail of missiles, one of the researchers noted tiny indentations in the fine-grained volcanic tuff. This led directly to the discovery of the "Laetoli Trackway" as the excavators re-focused their search for human or mammal prints rather than fossils.

The discoveries at both Laetoli and Olduvai were largely unearthed by chance. But were it not for the patient and dedicated pioneering work of two British archaeologists, Louis and Mary Leakey, such "accidents" might not have occurred in the first place.

Louis Leakey first visited Olduvai Gorge in 1931 and he and Mary dedicated 60 years of their lives to the search for fossils of early mankind. Their early living conditions were basic and very hot. Stores had to be brought from Kenya and water had to be carried several km on foot from Olmoti, an extinct volcano.

Mary Leakey first visited Olduvai in 1935 when she was 22 years old. It was not until 24 years later, on 17 July 1959 that she found *Zinjanthropus*, named *Austalopithecus boisei* after Charles Boise who had supported their work at Olduvai.

The skull had a concave, forward jutting face, poorly developed brow, a ridge above the eyes and large teeth. This hominid had been a vegetarian living off roots, nuts and seeds, had had no chin and a brain capacity about one-third of today. *Zinjanthropus* moved upright on two legs but had not lost the capacity to swing in trees.

Louis was unimpressed by Mary's find. It was that of a forebear of *Homo habilis* that they both believed had lived at Olduvai.

Louis (left) at Tendaguru dinosaur bed in southern Tanzania and Mary (right) at Olduvai with her pet Dalmatian dogs

In 1960 their eldest son, Jonathan, who had just left school, found by chance the jaw of *Homo habilis*, nicknamed the "Toolmaker". Then late that year Louis at last unearthed the remains of *Homo erectus*. The skull had double the brain cavity of the original *Zinjanthropus*. After 30 years, Leakeys' beliefs had been rewarded.

Olduvai's modern chronology

1911 Professor Wilhelm Kattwinkle stumbles on Olduvai Gorge
1913 Dr Hans Reck follows up Kattwinkle's find and maps the gorge
1918 Germany loses First World War and its African colonies
1931 Dr Louis Leakey's first of many visits to Olduvai Gorge
1931 First 700,000-year-old Acheulean handaxe found at Olduvai
1959 Mary Leakey finds Zinjanthopus, the "Nutcracker Man"
1960 Leakey's son, Jonathan, finds Olduvai's first Homo Habilis
1960 Louis Leakey excavates Olduvai's first Homo Erectus
1978 Laetoli's 3.6-million-year-old hominid footprints are found

Recently circumcised Maasai boy

Today the Maasai people live and herd their livestock in the area they call *Oldupai* after the endemic sisal that grows wild in the area. *"Ol"* means place of and *"dupai"* means sisal. As with many written African words, Europeans mispronounced this as "Olduvai".

SERENGETI NATIONAL PARK

Like an unbroken thread, the annual migration of the wildebeest and zebra binds the Serengeti's ecosystem much as it has done for the past two million years. Upon this migration, triggered by the rains, almost all things depend.

The annual pilgrimage involves some 1.5 million animals that must search for the grass and water they need to survive. During this spectacle the migration will cover some 3,200 km (2,000 miles) and devour 4,000 tonnes of grass a day. A quarter of a million animals will be born.

From about December to May, with some seasonal variations in time and scale, the migrating herds are on the short grass plains from Lake Ndutu past Naabi Hill. There they give birth and regain their strength.

Wildebeest bunching and drinking as they prepare to run the gauntlet of the waiting crocodiles as they cross the Grumeti River.

Brief profile

Declared a park in 1951 and extended in 1965
The word "Serengeti" originates from the Maasai language
In Maa the word "Siringet" means, "wide open plains"
It is Tanzania's largest park measuring 14,763 sq km
That is larger than Northern Ireland
Sukuma, Kurya, Dorobo and Maasai once shared the area
Maasai are the only truly nomadic pastoralists
The other people are agro-pastoralists
Serengeti is accessible by vehicle all the year round
The visitor bed capacity is strictly limited to 790
This is in tented camps, lodges, campsites and a hostel
Acacia, Terminalia and Commiphora trees dominate.

Opposite page: Lion cub

The plains become a cacophony of sound with the zebra making their familiar barking *kwa-ha-ha* calls and the wildebeest snorting loudly. Younger wildebeest show off their paces while older bulls rub their facial glands in the grass marking the border that other bulls should not cross.

But cross they do and a ritualistic battle for turf and females ensues. These battles rarely result in injuries, the fighting is seldom serious and any pretext is used to break off a confrontation.

In May, as water becomes the limiting factor on the short grass plains, hundreds of thousands of animals stretching over many kilometres head northwest. Simba and Moru areas then become the favourite places to watch them.

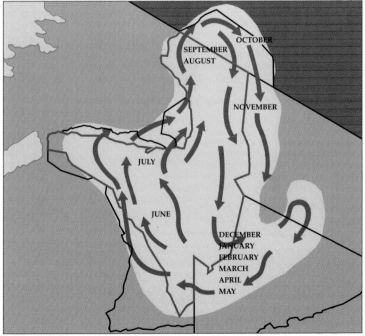

Migration routes

Zebras look both ways for potential danger

Inexplicably, despite their search for water, the migration swings northeast just before Lake Victoria, heading into neighbouring Kenya's Maasai Mara Game Reserve during September and October. Then they head south again, back to Tanzania to complete the circle to Serengeti's short grass plains where they began their journey 12 months earlier.

Such an exercise may appear senseless to the outsider. Flooded rivers have to be crossed where many animals will drown, calves will die or be lost crossing lakes. Disease, poachers and predators will contribute to thinning the herd.

Lions and other predators follow the migration picking off the weaker members and the calves. At the Grumeti River where the migration crosses the western corridor of the Serengeti, crocodiles lurk awaiting their annual feast.

This is part of what scientists starkly call "the food chain". It is a vast conveyor belt of plenty with the migration providing most of the food.

Other predators that lurk in the wings prefer smaller game to wildebeest and zebra. Leopards, often found in trees along the Seronera River, may haul as many as four or five Grant's or Thomson's gazelles into their leafy larders. There they are safe from the unwelcome attention of lions and hyenas.

Cheetahs, with their electrifying bursts of speed, chase similar prey. Baboons and jackals often eat the newborn calves of Thomson's. Vultures arrive on the kills within minutes, greedily and noisily disputing the meal.

Female cheetah

As the migration marches on, the plains that the wildebeest and zebra have left behind turn from green to brown while the rainclouds beckon ahead. The Thomson's and Grant's gazelle, the next most populous animals in the Serengeti, remain behind temporarily, grazing on the ample grass left by the migration and slaking their thirst on Sodom apples, a small yellow or green fruit that is common in East Africa.

Even storks and pelicans are beneficiaries of the migration. The animals trample the shallow pools they cross, and the mud clogs up the gills of fish. The fish surface to breathe and the patient birds are waiting.

The herds leave their imprint on the land, now crossed by a myriad of trails. In September, dry season fires sweep the Serengeti. The smaller reptiles and insects are driven ahead of the flames and picked off by waiting birds and other insectivores.

For the wildebeest and zebra, this is the low point in the migration. The landscape is blackened and devoid of grass, and a pall of smoke hangs in the air. But no matter the animals' weakened condition, they must escape the dustbowl to survive.

Vultures wheel overhead on the thermals, and predators, including the Serengeti's 6,500 hyenas, hunt down the weakened animals.

Marabou stork waiting for fish

Even in death, the wildebeest serve a purpose in nature's complex web. The bodies enrich the shallow lakes and rivers making it better for flamingoes and other wading birds. Their bleached bones provide camouflaged nesting sites for tiny plovers.

Spotted hyenas on a buffalo carcass

Thomson's gazelle (left) and Grant's gazelle

Not all the Serengeti's vast herds join the migration. Elephants around Ndutu and the northeastern Lobo area, giraffe, buffalo, eland, topi, kongoni, impala and other residents stay on as do many of the predators.

Apart from vultures that tend to follow the migration, the Serengeti's 517 identified bird species stay within their range. Some are migrants, found in the Serengeti only during the European winter months from October to April.

Others such as the ostrich, which is the largest bird and numbers some 4,300 in the Serengeti, are present all year round. So are the colourful Lilac-breasted rollers, the Kori bustard which is the largest flying bird in the park, Secretary birds and the Superb starling that is ever-present at the Naabi Hill entrance gate. There are also magnificently coloured Fischer's lovebirds with their orange-red faces, parrot-like beaks and bright green, almost translucent plumage.

In the Seronera area, at the centre of the park around the headquarters, visitors will notice many whistling thorn acacias. These have flourished in recent years as a result of the policy of controlled fires by burning early when the grass still has moisture.

This burning, done by park staff, begins in June and insulates the Serengeti from the harsher dry season fires that start outside the park and account for 75 percent of woodland depletion.

The whistling thorn acacias also have an intriguing symbiotic and protective relationship with the tiny cocktail ants. The ants live in the acacias' dark-skinned, bulbous galls and emerge with their tails exposed ready to strike the unwary.

The second protective mechanism of these acacias are the long, very sharp thorns. Even giraffes, with their puckered lips and long tongues, carefully skirt them as they graze on the tender green leaves between.

White-fronted bee-eater

Agama lizards, the males coloured red and blue during mating, are to be found around Seronera and on other rock *kopjes* as are diminutive hyrax. Nile monitor lizards are found along waterways where they prey on crocodile eggs.

Butterflies exist in abundance, particularly after the rains. Damp areas and stream banks are places butterflies most frequently drink and concentrations are to be found at puddles containing animal urine and dung.

Male agama lizard

The really nice thing about the Serengeti is that even at the height of the tourist season you can go all day without seeing another vehicle by leaving the beaten track. That alone makes the Serengeti very different and special.

TARANGIRE NATIONAL PARK

For many people who have spent years in the African bush, Tarangire is their favourite national park on Tanzania's richly endowed northern circuit.

Looking down from the high ridge, it is not difficult to see why; the Tarangire River winds away into the distance, through open, undulating country.

Brief profile

Tarangire National Park was established in 1970
Today the park is 2,642 sq km in size
June to February is the best time to visit
The park can sleep 266 people
Main roads are good and the landscape generally open
Over 517 species of birds exist
Trees include Acacia, Terminalia and Combretum
Grasses include Themeda triandra and Pennisetum mezianum

The Tarangire River, from which the park takes its name, runs through the park. It supplies Tarangire National Park's lifeblood and becomes the dry season magnet for the vast herds of wildlife that must come down to drink.

Elephants, as well as large herds of buffalo and Burchell's zebra come to the Tarangire River to drink during the dry season, while tall Maasai giraffe are visible as they make their way elegantly through the trees on the river's edge.

As the visitor watches the events unfolding below, Vervet monkeys and Unstriped ground squirrels play nearby.

Unstriped ground squirrel

Opposite page: View of the park down the Tarangire river

Baobabs

Baobab tree and fruit

Baobab trees, credited by legend as holding up the sky, can be found in many parts of Tarangire National Park. The elephantine trunks of these ungainly giants, appear disproportionate to their scraggy upper branches.

The trees are steeped in history, mythology and belief. Visitors may be offered the gourd-like fruit from the baobab tree. Try the contents; it is refreshing if somewhat bitter. The dry, powdery pulp contains appreciable quantities of tartaric acid and potassium bitartrate and is not poisonous.

Most of the tree has some uses. The torn bark on the trunks is where elephants have stripped the bark for food. The young leaves are edible and the fibrous wood is used for weaving and making rope. The trunks are hollow and act as reservoirs for water, while the trees attract wild bees and nesting hornbills.

It is said that God deliberately planted the baobab tree upside down so that you see the roots and not the branches. Another legend is that a lion will devour anyone rash enough to pluck a flower from the tree. A third is that the seeds soaked in water protect against crocodiles.

The first recorded attempt to date the baobab occurred in 1749 when a French botanist, Michel Adanson said that one at the mouth of the Senegal River was 5,150 years old. He later gave his name to the tree whose scientific name is Adansonia digita.

Tarangire National Park is just 118 km (74 miles) southwest of Arusha, the country's tourist hub, along the tarred Great North Road that proceeds to the country's political capital, Dodoma.

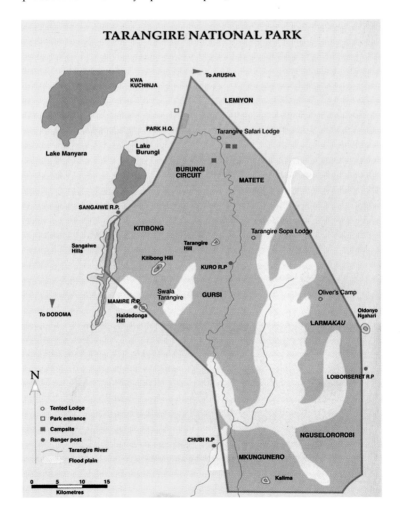

Tarangire is central to Tanzania's northern circuit of Arusha and Kilimanjaro national parks, and to Lake Manyara and Serengeti national parks, making it the perfect place to begin or end an African safari.

The park has been carefully zoned. The lodges that are popular with tourists are in the area mapped for general use. A tented camp is located in the semi-wilderness zone and this is truly a delightful escape.

A walking camp is located in the portion of the park set aside as wilderness. From this camp the visitor can leave the confines of a vehicle and undertake walking safaris with experienced guides.

Acacia trees at sunset

Less visible than the ubiquitous baobabs are the sausage trees found along watercourses, tamarind trees, *Acacia tortilis* otherwise known as "umbrella" trees that excellently frame a picture at sunset, and candelabra trees on the rocky slopes.

After the rains, the park is filled with a mixture of indigenous flowers. *Ipomoea hildebranatii* dominates. With its distinct purple lines from the centre to the edges of the white petals, this flower is commonly found in grassland with scattered *Acacia* and *Acacia-Commiphora* deciduous bushland.

Two other common flowers are members of the hibiscus family. The common hibiscus has yellow petals with a red centre, while the marsh hibiscus is purple.

Ipomoea hildebranatii (above) Marsh hibiscus (below)

Apart from 6,500 elephants (the largest number in northern Tanzania) as well as zebra, white-bearded wildebeest and buffalo, what really sets Tarangire apart is its landscape and birdlife.

More than 500 different species have been recorded in the park and these include Bateleur eagles that wheel lazily overhead on the thermals. The bateleur eagle in flight is distinguishable by its black feathers, short tail, red legs and beak.

Often perched in trees are tawny eagles while a wide range of goshawks, sparrowhawks and falcons hunt throughout Tarangire.

Guinea fowl, the ubiquitous chickens of Africa, gather in large flocks, quelea birds whirr noisily overhead seeking new seed-bearing plants on which to feed, while yellow-necked spurfowl mingle with their cousins, francolins, beside the road.

At the Engelhard Bridge that crosses the Tarangire River, lesser-striped swallows roost on the parapet, while egrets peer fixedly at the water seeking their next meal.

The Tarangire ecosystem encompasses the southern Maasai Steppe. This extensive ecosystem covers an area of some 35,000 sq km and is 13 times the size of the national park.

Tarangire National Park cuts into the southwestern side of the Maasai Steppe. It is the fifth biggest park in Tanzania and contains large areas of wetlands such as those found in the Gursi, Larmakua and Nguselorobi swamps and at Silale.

Lesser-striped swallows

Egret sets off the granite rocks in the Taringire River at Engelhard Bridge

These wetlands act as sponges supplying the Tarangire River during the dry season from late May until October, and rarely dry up.

The park lies in the eastern portion of the Great Rift Valley and is dominated by three types of rock formations: pre-Cambrian gneiss that forms the park's basement and gives rise to the *kopjes* (rock outcrops) that distinguish Tarangire.

The main soil types in Tarangire are well-drained red loams, those originating from lake deposits and sediments, and black-cotton soil that is characterized by its low organic content and has an accumulation of calcium carbonate developed from lava under the humid, tropical climate.

Apart from elephant, zebra, wildebeest, buffalo and giraffe, Tarangire contains almost the full range of animals found in east Africa. During the wet season, these animals disperse outside the park where calving takes place.

Climate

Tarangire is located in a semi-arid area and is characterized by brief phases of rain followed by a prolonged dry season that can last up to seven months.

The annual average rainfall during the erratic short rains in November and December, and the longer and heavier rains from mid-March to late May, is around 650mm (26 inches).

The dry season minimum temperature is 16 degrees C in June and July while the peak of 27 degrees C occurs in December to February.

Regal male lions

Lion, leopard, cheetah, hyena, African wild dog, bat-eared fox, black-backed jackal, civet, serval cat and several species of mongoose are all included among Tarangire's carnivores. Lions are plentiful and leopards may be seen occasionally in trees, but cheetah are uncommon.

Bushbuck, lesser and greater kudu, eland, Coke's hartebeest or Kongoni, Kirk's dik-dik, duiker, Thomson's and Grant's gazelle, gerenuk, fringe-eared oryx, impala, steinbok, Bohor reedbuck and waterbuck have all been sighted and there are many warthogs.

Conspicuous absentees include rhinoceros, wiped out in the poaching scourge in the 1970s and 1980s, and hippopotamus that have been killed for their meat and fat or have wisely relocated.

Apart from Arusha National Park that has its own charm, Tarangire is the least known and visited of northern Tanzania's national parks. That may be its greatest blessing, making tourist traffic light.

Black-backed jackal

MAFIA ISLAND MARINE PARK
& KILWA

Mafia Island is only a 30-minute flight south of the commercial capital of Dar es Salaam and 20 km off the Tanzanian coastline. Chole Bay and Kitutia Reef, two of Tanzania's eight offshore marine reserves declared in 1975, are incorporated into the marine park.

Because of the small size of the eight original reserves, coupled with limited financial and human resources, it was recognized that they existed only on paper. Dynamite fishing and coral exploitation continued unabated.

But Tanzania, with 800 km of coastline, recognized its high dependence upon marine resources. There followed an alternative proposal to establish larger marine areas that reduced the traditional conflicts between conservation and livelihoods. Now, about 18,000 people live in 14 villages wholly or partially within the park.

Mafia Island Marine Park was officially declared in November 1994. Since it was passed by parliament under the Marine Parks and Reserves Act, a second marine park has been added at Mnazi Bay just south of the port of Mtwara, close to the Mozambique border.

The sea around Mafia hosts an outstanding mosaic of tropical marine habitats ranging through coral reefs, seagrass beds, mangroves and inter-tidal flats. Most of the marine park is less than 20 metres below mean tide levels.

Pair of Long-nosed butterfly fish (above) and a Coral or Jewel grouper

Extensive inter-tidal flats stretch along the southern part of Mafia Island, around Chole and Juani Islands, and between Jibondo Island and Kitutia Reef. A channel, 20 to 30 metres deep, carries tidal water through the Kinasi Pass and Chole Bay as far as the Chole channel.

Opposite page: Colourful fish swim amidst the coral

The main ocean current is the permanent north-flowing East African Coastal Current. This can reach a speed of 4.5 knots during the peak months (June/July) of the southeast monsoon *(kusi)*.

The flow of the current is interrupted by the park's islets and reefs, and is strongly influenced by diurnal tidal currents generated by a tidal range of up to four metres. The sheltered western side of Mafia Island, where there are better beaches, is heavily influenced by its proximity to the mainland.

In contrast, the eastern side is exposed to the full force of the Indian Ocean although it is somewhat protected by a 33-km-long outer reef that stretches along the full extent of this seaboard.

The main outer fringe of this reef is gently sloping and dominated by hard corals. The outer part of Kinasi Pass is characterized by shallow platforms dominated by soft coral and algae, giving way to dramatically vertical reef walls that bottom out onto sandy platforms 20 to 50 metres in depth. Thereafter it steeply shelves into the Indian Ocean.

The south of Chole Bay has highly diverse topographic structures and hydrology, and the highest hard coral and other reef species found in this area. Other sheltered sub-tidal areas to the west are less rich in species but are notable for their shallow algae and coralline reef platforms and sandy areas studded with coral outcrops.

Habitat distribution, levels of disturbance and diversity vary greatly between the eastern and western sectors of the park with Chole Bay

and the outer parts of Kinasi Pass having greater habitat diversity, larger numbers of species and being less disturbed. The deeper reef walls in Chole Bay and on the outer reef are comparatively pristine.

The presence of mangroves, seagrass beds, algae, sponge and soft coral beds, as well as the fringing coral reef and adjacent algae-dominated coral reef outside Kinasi Pass, means that Chole Bay contains examples of the majority of tropical marine ecosystems.

Divers

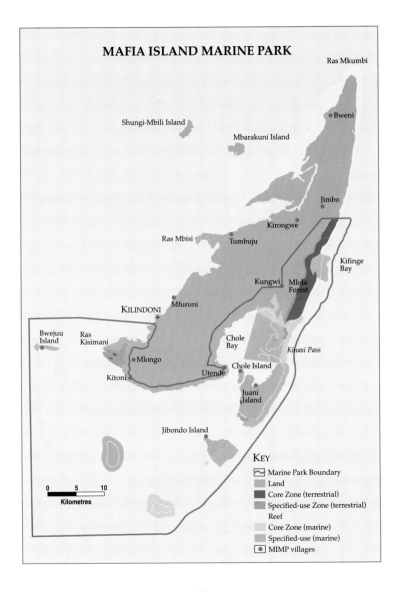

MAFIA ISLAND MARINE PARK

Ras Mkumbi

Bweni

Shungi-Mbili Island

Mbarakuni Island

Jimbo

Kirongwe

Ras Mbisi   Tumbuju

Kifinge
Bay

Kungwi   Mlola
Forest

KILINDONI   Mfuruni

Bwejuu   Ras
Island   Kisimani   Chole
Bay   Kinasi Pass

Mlongo   Chole Island

Kitoni   Utende

Juani
Island

Jibondo Island

KEY

⬦ Marine Park Boundary
  Land
  Core Zone (terrestrial)
  Specified-use Zone (terrestrial)
  Reef
  Core Zone (marine)
  Specified-use (marine)
◉ MIMP villages

0   5   10
Kilometres

For the expert and the novice diver or snorkeller, Mafia Island Marine Park offers dramatic underwater viewing with a wide variety of choices only 30 minutes from the hotel. Visibility is 20 to 25 metres from October to February dropping to 5 to 10 metres from June and September.

Fire, staghorn and foliose corals afford a sanctuary for a colourful range of fish from angel to wrasse. Fusiliers, coris, rainbow runners, jack, rays may all be found, while further offshore tuna, cobia, kingfish, mackerel, bonito and turtles are included as well as a few "dangerous" fish. Sensible behaviour combined with local knowledge will minimize the risks.

Over 2,000 species of fish from 150 families exist in the western Indian Ocean and new species are being identified. Whether diving or snorkeling, their behaviour, colours, relationships to each other and to other marine organisms are an endless source of fascination.

Historically, Mafia Island was once part of the Zanzibar archipelago with the two northern islands of Pemba and Unguja (which today make up Zanzibar) forming the bulk of the remainder. However, geographically Mafia is part of the Songosongo archipelago.

This domain was part of the colonial empire of the Omani Sultan of Zanzibar. In recognition of the sultan's claim, the British did not incorporate the island as part of mainland Tanganyika until November 1922, four years after they took over the colony from Germany after that country's defeat in the First World War.

Lying in the Indian Ocean, Mafia Island faces the multiple deltas of the Rufiji River near the final resting place of the German cruiser, the *Konigsberg*, while further inland lies Africa's largest game reserve, the Selous.

Two-bar anemone fish and Soft thistle coral

The people of Mafia call themselves Mafians and not *mafioso*. The population of Mafia is just over 45,000 and the island is 48 km long and 17 km wide. The vast majority are Muslims whose economic activities include harvesting cashew and coconuts, fishing and tourism.

Tourism on Mafia is still very low but growing. At least four beach resorts for tourists exist and there are self-catering and cheaper cottages near the district capital of Kilindoni. Commercial planes fly regularly to and from Kilindoni while there are also charter planes and slower sea transport.

Coconut trees comprising of African Talls and Malaysian Dwarfs dominate the Mafia skyline. The trees have been imported to Mafia since the 19th century but today there is only one commercial coconut plantation with 200,000 palms on the island.

Interspersed among the coconut palms are cashew trees, although few are sprayed to prevent fungal infection. Cassava, imported from Brazil to feed slaves during Portugal's 200-year tenure in the Indian Ocean, is the island's main subsistence crop.

Climate

Mafia Island has slightly acidic, loamy and sandy soil, and receives almost 2,000 mm of rain a year. It is therefore only suitable for growing coconuts and cashews as commercial export crops. The island's temperature rarely drops below 20 degrees C or rises above 33 degrees C.

The Indian Ocean monsoons affect the climate. The northeast monsoon (kaskazi) blows from November to March and the more vigorous southeast monsoon (kusi) from April until August. An intermediate easterly monsoon (matlai) occurs in September/October.

Cashew nuts ripening on the tree; coconut palms called African talls

Fishing is the main offshore activity for a substantial number of the population although domestic consumption of fish on Mafia is relatively small. The fish used to be sun-dried on the island and shipped by sailing dhow to the mainland coastal markets of Tanzania.

In the 1980s this began to change with the introduction of outboard motors and ice. Commercial fish traders from the mainland began to arrive on the spring tide packing their two-tonne iceboxes at sea direct from the fishing boats and transporting the catch to market. As a result, fewer fish are landed for local consumption.

The establishment of the marine park has curtailed some of the more environmentally damaging activities. In the 1990s, 90 tonnes of live sea coral and fossilized coral rock were taken from the marine park to build houses. Mangrove poles were also extracted to build boats, as building poles and as firewood.

For the tourist, Chole Mjini is well worth a visit. Some 1,200 flying foxes (bats) roost in the giant trees by day, flying in search of flowers and fruit at dusk. These bats are harmless to humans.

Battuta would have mounted the steps at Husuni Kubwa (Swahili for large fort) from a boat similar to that in the background.

Kilwa

The ancient city state of Kilwa is only 10 minutes further south by plane. "Amongst the most beautiful of cities, and elegantly built," was the description by Ibn Battuta who arrived at Kilwa in 1331.

Battuta's written record in Arabic is probably the earliest surviving eyewitness account of the Tanzanian coastline. Battuta, a Berber lawyer from Morocco, also visited China and India, traveled further than Marco Polo and is better known in the Arabic-speaking world.

He had met the Sultan of Kilwa, Al Hassan ibn Suleiman, during the latter's two-year sojourn at Mecca to study spiritual science. "Should you be in my neck of the woods…" one can imagine the Sultan saying to Battuta at Mecca. The rest is history.

Battuta describes the city, its gardens, orchards and the mosque. The palace had many rooms and open courtyards as well as a circular swimming pool. Below the cliff was a gradually descending slope where boats would anchor. At the palace, Battuta would have dined off Chinese tableware, a symbol of wealth in Kilwa (Quiloa).

To build and maintain an establishment such as this would have required a large number of labourers or slaves. This slavery (that Battuta called a "Holy War") was conducted by the Sultan in armed forays against the Muli (Moori), as they called the people of the mainland.

Visiting Hindu and Muslim merchants trading in items ranging from cloth to rice,

Standing columns of Kilwa's Great Mosque

and their servants, mingled with slaves on the streets. Lodging rooms for trading were provided near Kilwa's mosque.

The nearby Great Mosque, built later with its elaborate five aisles, columns (many of which are still standing) and ornate domed ceilings, was then the envy of other settlements along the coast.

SAADANI & BAGAMOYO

Saadani is set to become Tanzania's first national park fronting onto the ocean and if the visitors are really lucky they may see lions and elephants - or their tracks - in the sand. The number of species of animals in the park will amaze visitors.

This national park will be the closest one to Dar es Salaam's rapidly expanding population. Therein lies its natural market once the Wami River is forded and the road is upgraded, like the tarred road from Dar es Salaam to Bagamoyo. On the way to Saadani, the visitor can call in at the Kaole Ruins just before Bagamoyo or stay in the famous town.

Brief profile

Saadani National Park is to be declared in 2004/5
It is roughly 1,178 sq km in size
The area is sparsely populated
It comprises of Zaraninge forest and coastal villages
As well as Mkwaja North and South former ranches
It faces the Indian Ocean between Bagamoyo and Tanga
Saadani is 40 km from the Zanzibar island of Unguja

To the south of Saadani and 45 km away, lies the historic slave town of Bagamoyo. To the north is Pangani, once a lesser-known slave outlet and an explorer starting point. To the west is the Chalinze-to-Segera tarred south-north highway off which the motorist turns at Mandera village just after the bridge fording the Wami River.

The land at Saadani rises to only 350 metres and the park will incorporate the current game reserve, the northern and southern sections of the former Mkwaja Ranch, a salt works where pelicans and flamingos may be seen, forest reserves, village land, railways and roads.

The park will also incorporate the Zaraninge forest and forested patches of Mkwaja Ranch. In this habitat, Saadani's 50-strong elephant population is most frequently found, either along the Msangazi River or the watersheds of rivers such as the Wami, Pangani and Mvave, or sometimes in coastal villages.

Opposite page: Hippopotamuses in the Wami River

Hippopotamus exist in large numbers, particularly along the Wami River, and a boat trip is well worthwhile. The visitor may also see crocodiles and the much smaller Nile monitor lizards that feed on the eggs laid by crocodiles.

Reedbuck in dense vegetation

Sightings of both reedbuck and bushbuck are more frequent at Saadani than elsewhere in Tanzania's parks. The more numerous reedbuck are found along rivers and lakes while bushbuck are to be found, as their name suggests, in the bush.

They are very similar in body and horn size, and both hide in patches of cover. Their presence at Saadani probably reflects the balance between savanna and forest vegetation for which dry season fire is an essential ingredient to palatable re-growth for both species.

Among the larger species, there are 200 giraffe that consume taller vegetation promoting a nutrient cycle that accelerates food production for the smaller animals, and some 100 grass-eating buffalo that also play an important role in the overall dynamics of the ecosystem.

White-bearded wildebeest

Lions, leopards, hyenas, genets, civets and other predators exist at Saadani and there are large numbers of waterbucks, zebras, warthogs, bushpigs, yellow baboons, black-and-white colobus monkeys (most easily seen along the Wami River), vervet and blue monkeys, often referred to as Sykes.

The dry country, White-bearded wildebeest similar to those found in the Serengeti, were introduced to Saadani from northern Tanzania. At present it is uncertain what impact this expanding population will have on the 1,000 Lichenstein's hartebeest at Saadani.

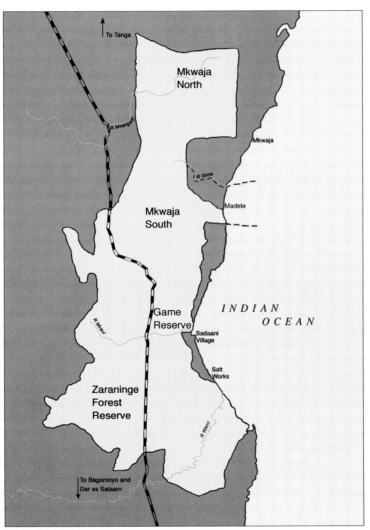

Map of Saadani

The wildebeest have expanded in the flatter parts of Saadani where there has been little management of the water supplies, while the hartebeest, identifiable by their thick and short "S" shaped horns, are to be found along drainage-line grassland in woodlands that contain at least two plant communities, access to water and a firm footage.

The other noteworthy species found at Saadani is the scimitar-horned, glossy, black-coated Roosevelt sable. Previously they were thought to exist only in Kenya's Shimba Hills, where the relic population of 120 is listed as "endangered".

But DNA tests have now linked both the Saadani and Shimba populations with some 12,000 Roosevelt sable in the Selous Game Reserve to the south. This animal was named after the American President who visited Tanzania early in the 20th century.

The main habitats within the Saadani ecosystem are along the Wami and Msangazi rivers, the entire catchment area of the Mvave River, Mkwaja Ranch, on open land on the escarpment overlooking the coastal plains, and on the shoreline including the mangroves and the turtle-nesting sites.

Madete Green Turtle Breeding Beach, 13 km from Mkwaja village, is one of the most important breeding places for this endangered species since Maziwi Island off Pangani succumbed to erosion and vanished into the Indian Ocean in the early 1990s.

Turtles have a homing instinct that sees them migrating thousands of miles on their pilgrimage back to the site of their birth. One found in Tanzanian waters had been tagged 2,000 km away in South Africa.

Sea turtle

At Maziwi Island some 200 to 300 green turtles used to breed annually before that nesting site submerged. As a result the Madete project, largely the initiative of Geoff Fox, the former manager of Mkwaja Ranch, has become doubly important.

Turtles copulate at sea but give birth on the land. The female turtle digs a nest on the beach, often above the high water mark. Into this nest she may lay 100 eggs before covering them and returning to the sea.

Incubation takes two months with temperatures determining the sex of offspring who must scuttle for the sea avoiding birds, ghost crabs and other predators. Few complete the journey.

For those who do, the sea poses new hazards, not least of them humans who eat turtle meat, buy their eggs as a delicacy and use their shells to fashion into combs. Tourists buy young turtles as "decorative items" and some turtle portions are used for medicinal purposes.

Saadani's soil texture is generally fine with the lower lying basins comprising of coastal saline clay while further inland there is dark cracking clay. Even in a four-wheel drive vehicle it is easy to get bogged down and the park is closed during the height of the rains from March to mid-May.

There are few rocky slopes, while the dune ridges along the foreshore are low and barely distinguishable. Drainage, even on sloping ground, is poor and the best-drained surface area is found on the edge of escarpment. Most watercourses are sandy and dry on the surface with perennial water below.

Warthogs are numerous at Saadani, particularly on the former Mkwaja ranches

While the geology shows signs of recent marine sediments, including an abundance of clay, there is very little sign of coral rag such as that found on Zanzibar. The alluvial deposits on the floodplains and in the estuaries are very recent.

Climate

Saadani is typical of equatorial coastal east Africa. There are two rainy seasons a year that bring an average rainfall of about 1,000 mm (40 inches). The rainfall is less at the coast and higher inland.

The main wet months are in April and May with lighter showers in November and December and immediately preceding the heavier rains. February is generally the hottest month although in other months the temperature will be above 25 degrees C.

The air at Saadani is very humid accounting for the lichen on trees over 25 years in age. This is particularly true near the coastline.

Bagamoyo

Bagamoyo (and to a lesser extent Pangani) was once the gateway for merchants trading with the Swahili people of the coast, the exit point for slaves and ivory from the interior, and the entry point for European explorers of the "dark continent", as all of Africa was then known.

Kaole, only an hour's walk to the south, preceded Bagamoyo. The Shirazis arrived there from Persia in the 13th century, about 500 years after the first Arab settlements, introducing embryonic Islam. Kaole was abandoned after its heyday in the 14th and 15th centuries and today consists of a series of tombs and ancient ruins.

Kaole Ruins today (left) and a tomb (right)

There followed 200 years of Portuguese presence in the Indian Ocean followed by Omani occupation. The Germans and finally the British colonized the area.

Abushiri ibn Salim al-Harthi, a wealthy sugar plantation owner from Pangani, and Heri bin Juma, an African chief from Saadani, tried to end the cycle of colonization with a revolt known as the Bushiri uprising. The German colonizers captured and hanged Bushiri at Pangani in 1889.

From Bagamoyo, a Catholic priest, Father Gomminger, wrote to a friend in Europe: "You may call the east Africans rebels, but they are not. They only did what everyone in every nation would have done, what we would have done. They fight for their freedom and their rights." Therein lies a message for today's "liberators".

From the days when it was called *"Bwagamoyo"*, the town has lapsed into decay and relative slumber although parts of it are now being rehabilitated. *Bwaga* means to "rest" or the "end of a journey" while *moyo* is the "heart" in Swahili, hence the loose translation of "lay down your heart".

Most of the slaves were transported to Zanzibar's "slave market" where they were prodded and poked before being sold like animals. This prompted Scottish missionary, David Livingstone to record: "...for every slave sold on the auction block in Zanzibar or nearby ports, five others died during the journey getting there."

Although Livingstone's name is inextricably linked with Bagamoyo, he never visited the town during his lifetime. It was only after his death in Zambia on 1 May 1873 that two of his guides, Chuma and Susi, carried his body 1,500 km to Bagamoyo.

There it lay in the chapel of the French Holy Ghost Fathers who five years earlier had been given land by the Omani Sultan of Zanzibar (who claimed all of the land) to build a mission station. The missionaries built a village for freed slaves, a giant cross on the foreshore to mark their landing place, a school and a workshop.

Despite being Bagamoyo's most visible and vocal presence today, the Victorian message of the Christian missionaries did nothing to contain the march of Islam - over 85 percent of those on the coast today are Muslims.

Many of the people the visitor will meet at Saadani, Bagamoyo and Pangani are the descendents of slaves. Today they make a precarious livelihood from fishing and subsistence agriculture while remembering the past of their ancestors inland.

This boma (fort) at Bagamoyo was built in 1897 and was the residence of the German colonial governor. Now it is one of several buildings in Bagamoyo undergoing reconstruction.

ZANZIBAR

Age and distance separate Zanzibar's two main islands. Unguja emerged as an island only 7 million years ago; before then you could walk to the island 40 km east of Bagamoyo that is separated from the mainland by a shallow channel.

Eighty km to the north of Unguja is Pemba, which emerged some 27 million years ago. It is 80 km east of Tanga and is separated by a channel up to 800 metres deep. Pemba was also once joined to mainland Africa.

Zanzibar

Unguja and Pemba were first settled by Africans
Next came the Shirazis fleeing persecution in Persia
They were followed by the Omani Arabs
The Portuguese ruled the Indian Ocean for 200 years
After stiff competition, Zanzibar became a British colony
On 10 December 1963, Zanzibar became nominally independent
But the British ensured that an Omani Sultan was Head of State
On 12 January 1964, the Africans overthrew the Omani hegemony
That day is celebrated as the Zanzibar Revolution.

Unguja means "transit" and is often referred to as Zanzibar because that is where Zanzibar town is located. Unguja is a "continental island". Pemba is an "ancient continental island" with calm and translucent waters and some of the finest fishing and diving in the world.

Both are low-lying, mildly undulating islands fringed by some 50 smaller islands, none rising more than 200 metres above sea level. Coconut palms dominate the skyline and pristine beaches ring the islands. Mangrove trees guard many of the beaches from erosion and protect fish breeding grounds.

Opposite page: Lateen sail fishing dhow off Zanzibar

Deserted Zanzibar beach

The ancient water well at Unguja Ukuu

At Kizimkazi in the south of Unguja, snorkelers play with the dolphins while Nungwi aquarium in the north of the island is the best place to find sea turtles. Offshore, big-game fishers pursue sailfish and blue marlin. Tuna, kingfish, snapper and grouper are among the many fish available and for those who prefer their fish on plates, Zanzibar's restaurants and hotels cater for all tastes.

In addition to Unguja and Pemba being islands, this geographical classification contains another common word; they are "continental", in other words they are part of Africa. That Africans were the islands' first inhabitants is evident from historical and archaeological evidence, such as the water well still operating at Unguja Ukuu, where locally made iron tools from the 1st century have been excavated.

The early African, pre-Islamic inhabitants of Zanzibar arrived by boat from the mainland. They settled in coastal areas, relying on agriculture and fishing for their livelihoods. Domestic animals were few.

The eldest male of the family headed the community. As communities expanded into villages, clan leadership and collective ruling councils evolved. Members of the ruling councils were noted for their wisdom, bravery, tolerance and communal action.

These African settlements traded with the earliest mariners from the Arab world, India and China. Kizimkazi Dimbani on the southern tip of Unguja is one of the earliest known African settlements on the island and was particularly notable for its fine seafood.

The sea

Visitors will see an array of boats, some of which will be unfamiliar. Zanzibar has four basic types of traditional craft: the dugout canoes (mtumbwi), canoes with outriggers (ngalawa), inshore dhows (mashua) and the majestic ocean-going dhows (jahazi).

The dugout canoe, ideally hewn from a hollowed mango tree trunk, may have only 50 cm of draft. This is the most basic and oldest boat in the world. Canoes with outriggers are twice as long, measuring six metres and having double the draft.

An ocean-going dhow sailing from Zanzibar

Inshore dhows have a long forward overhang, raised bridge and an open section for carrying cargo. The ocean-going dhow is a larger version of this. Lateen-rigged boats are identifiable by their triangular sails extended by a long spar that sits low on the mast.

Lateen sails were adopted from Arab mariners. Few of the boats have modern navigational aids, sailors being guided by the stars and the smell of land. Longevity of boats is particularly important, locally made hardwood lasts for up to 20 years.

Writing in about 1220 AD, one mariner described Unguja as being "a large island in the land of Zenj [an Arabic word for black], in which is the seat of the King of Zenj. Ships make their way to it from all quarters."

The Shirazis from Persia began arriving in Zanzibar around the 10th century and unlike the earliest (as well as later) traders, they severed ties with their homeland and married African women. The ruling party of Zanzibar was previously called the Afro-Shirazi Party (ASP) in recognition of this reality.

A Swahili (coastal) culture began to emerge and scattered communities became more integrated. Embryonic Islam, probably spread by early mariners and traders, began about two centuries before the arrival of the Shirazis.

Little trace remains of Portugal's almost 200-year occupation of the Indian Ocean from 1503. A 16th century fortified dwelling at Mvuleni-Fukuchani in the northeast of Unguja and a pair of bronze cannons with the Portuguese royal coat of arms that were captured by the Persians, are among the few visible symbols of this period of colonization.

But the evidence of the Omani occupation after their defeat of Portugal is almost everywhere: in the narrow, cobbled streets of Zanzibar's Old Town, the Arabesque architecture, at the old fort, the museum and the ornate House of Wonders on the waterfront built by Sultan Barghash bin Said.

From 1698 until 12 January 1964 the Omani sultans ruled Zanzibar, leaving an indelible scar on the people. Slavery, forced labour, exploitation and deprivation were all hallmarks of this period. And ironically, it was the introduction of clove trees to the islands that brought with it increased demand for slaves.

House of Wonders

Slavery was rooted in the labour demands of the plantation economy in Zanzibar, throughout the Indian Ocean, the West Indies and elsewhere. Prior to the arrival of the Omanis, Zanzibar imported some 8,000 slaves a year. In the 1860s, this figure rose to 50,000-70,000 a year, with many more dying before reaching the coast.

One of the most infamous slavers of this period was a friend of David Livingstone. Nicknamed "Tippu Tip", his real name was Hamed bin Mohammed el Marjebi and he owned seven plantations and had 10,000 slaves. His house in Zanzibar town is said to be haunted and is given a wide berth.

Spices

Zanzibar once produced over 90 percent of the world's cloves, three-quarters of this on Pemba. Cloves, deriving from the French word clou (a nail), were introduced to the island in 1812 from the French possession of Bourbon (now Reunion). The Sultan decreed that three clove trees must be planted for every coconut tree.

Cloves

Cloves are the bud from the harvest and some trees are now 150 years old. The buds are separated from the stems before being dried on palm leaf mats. The best quality buds are retained for cooking, pickling, and the making of wines and spirits. The stems are used to make oil for flavouring tea, sweet and savoury dishes and in rice and cakes.

While Zanzibar is mainly known for cloves, the islands produce about 50 other spices. These include aniseed, bay leaves, black pepper, cardamom, chilli, cinnamon, coriander, cumin, curry leaves, dill seeds, fennel, garlic, ginger, lemon grass and turmeric.

A treaty signed in 1798 marked the beginning of formal relations between Britain and Oman. It was a document of convenience to both sides. The Sultan of Oman sought a militarily powerful ally to consolidate his shaky hold over the Persian Gulf and to combat the recalcitrant Mazrui family in the Kenyan city of Mombasa.

Zanzibar is famous for its ornate carved doors

Then at war with France, Britain wanted to prevent the planned march by Emperor Napoleon Bonaparte to seize the wealth of India. Furthermore, in 1772 Britain had formally outlawed slavery and it sought to replicate this in Oman. A number of British sailors died trying to enforce the prohibition and some of them are buried on Chapwani (or Grave) Island off Zanzibar Town.

The British did not wish to undermine the Omani Sultan of Zanzibar economically and a policy of "gradualism" was pursued. But Britain was turning the screw and Zanzibar was given formal "protectorate" status making it in effect a British colony.

Britain continued to perceive Zanzibar as an Arab outpost and the Omani Sultan was retained. Not until 1946 did the Legislative Council, headed by the British Resident, nominate an African member. Then in July 1963, the European power blatantly rigged the elections to prevent the ASP (that had won 54.21 percent of the vote) from taking power.

At the independence of Zanzibar on 10 December 1963, Britain installed the Sultan as head of state. Thirty-three days later, the Zanzibar Revolution occurred. The African majority, frustrated by almost 500 years of exploitation and recent electoral gerrymandering, finally took their destiny into their own hands.

Today few visitors bypass the islands' fruit. A bunch of over 100 bananas costs just US$3, fibreless mangoes come in 10 varieties and *shoki-shoki* (litchis) grow wild in bunches on trees where the bright red fruit looks like an unpeeled horse chestnut. These, and much more, are available in markets or on the roadside.

Carrageenan, obtained from seaweed and used extensively in the pharmaceutical industry, is one of Zanzibar's newer exports. A "gift from the ocean" is the way the islands' seaweed farmers describe this easy-to-grow crop. At least one hotel has seaweed salad on its menu and tourists can participate in the harvesting.

The economy of Zanzibar today is based on tourism. Its beautiful deserted beaches, the former slave market, Stone Town with its narrow, cobbled streets and plentiful souvenirs, the spice route, Jozani Forest and the Zanzibar red colobus monkeys are all high on the tourist itinerary.

Zanzibar still retains a remarkable degree of the past melded with the realities of the present and these two factors can only enhance your enjoyment. Coming from an island and understanding the history of subjugation, helps to comprehend the realities of today's Zanzibar beyond the romantic notions of childhood.

Bunches of shoki-shoki in Zanzibar market

Zanzibar red colobus monkey

Jozani National Park

Lying in a shallow trough on the fossil coral bedrock, this mature tropical forest is an hour's drive southeast of Zanzibar Town. Most visitors go to Jozani to see the conspicuous Zanzibar red colobus monkeys, 13 species of red colobus being found in Africa.

The seasonal flooding, wooded freshwater lake and very high watertable, are vital components of this unique forest swamp. A boardwalk takes visitors into the mangrove forest and there is also a nature trail where guides show Zanzibar's rich and diverse environmental mosaic. On the permanently wet trail, Oil Palms, Walking Palms, Raffia Palms and Wild Date Palms will all be seen.

KITULO PLATEAU

Kitulo is variously known as *Bustani ya Mungu* (Swahili for "God's Garden"), the "Serengeti of Flowers" or as "One of the great floral spectacles of the world", according to renowned artist and zoologist Jonathan Kingdon.

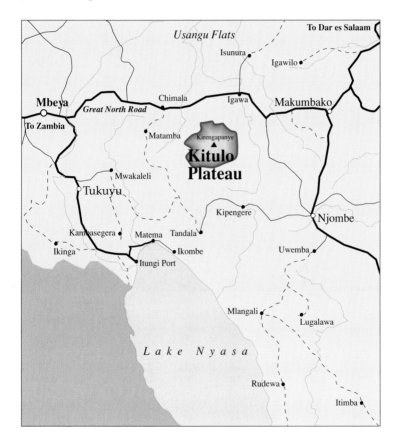

Opposite page: This brilliantly coloured Disa walleri is a member of the very extended orchid family.

Kitulo

Kitulo is to become a park to protect its floral diversity
It will be the first area in Africa protected for its unique flowers
The government announced that the park would be 402 sq km
Kitulo is best visited from January to May during the rains
But the roads and tracks are slippery at this time of the year
Almost 2,000 species of flowers occur in the Southern Highlands
Many species of flora and fauna are endemic to this area
Flowers include ground orchids, red-hot pokers, gladioli and irises
Birds include Blue swallow, Denham's bustard and many others
Southern Highlands colobus monkeys exist on the plateau's edge.

The Kitulo Plateau lies to the east of the southern agricultural town of Mbeya and is part of the Uporoto and Kipengere Range of the Southern Highlands, north of Lake Nyasa that is shared by Malawi, Mozambique and Tanzania. The area is recognized for its outstanding botanical importance as many of its flowers are endemic to the area.

Red flowering Disa Erubescens, another member of the orchid family

For longer than anyone can remember, people who live in some parts of Zambia, in northern Malawi and southwestern Tanzania have eaten the boiled roots of ground orchids, principally of the *Disa, Habenaria* and *Satyrium* genera.

The tubers are harvested, dried, pounded, boiled with baking soda or wood ash, and then served as a staple. Alternatively, the mixture is cooled and squeezed to remove the moisture before storage. The taste is rather like a meatless sausage, Zambians say.

Called *chikanda* in Zambia – where they are often advertised as "African prunes" – and *kinaka* in Tanzania, orchid tubers were once a traditional village delicacy, with the harvests of orchid tubers posing no threat to the reproductive ability of those growing in Tanzania.

In Zambia's urban areas, food shortages and the resulting commercialisation of the trade rose in the 10 years when President Frederick Chiluba was in power, destroying the traditional orchid areas in neighbouring countries and threatening others with extinction.

Interestingly, while the Zambian demand rose dramatically, that of Tanzania (where the orchid tubers are eaten in some areas in times of famine) has declined. Indeed in Tanzania, the young people no longer follow the eating habits of past generations.

These disclosures are contained in a paper published in early 2003 in *Oryx*, the International Journal of Conservation, Flora and Fauna published by Cambridge University Press. The authors are Dr Tim Davenport, Director of Tanzania's Southern Highlands Conservation Programme, a project of the Wildlife Conservation Society, and Tanzanian botanist Dr Henry Ndangalasi.

In the abstract of their article they say: "...the past decade has witnessed a dramatic rise in demand in Zambia, particularly in urban areas. This has triggered a burgeoning commercial market and has now prompted traders to seek tubers from Tanzania's Southern Highlands, an important centre of endemism for upland species of orchids."

The result is that Tanzania has decided to declare Kitulo, part of the Southern Highlands, as the country's fourteenth national park. This will increase the area that Tanzania has set aside for conservation to over 28 percent of the total land area of the country of 945,166 sq km. This is the highest percentage in the world.

View of Kitulo through flowers

Unlike Tanzania's famous Serengeti Plains or Ngorongoro Crater that are set aside to conserve the wildlife, or Mount Kilimanjaro that climbers seek to conquer, Kitulo is primarily to preserve the unique landscape and wild flowers from agricultural encroachment, particularly of commercial potato and pyrethrum farms, and orchid harvesters.

In southwestern Tanzania, collectors are now harvesting an estimated 2.2 to 4.1 million orchid tubers a year and as many as 85 species of orchids may be at risk. Large areas in Ufipa, Mbeya and Kipengere have already been stripped of terrestrial wild orchids with profound implications for the country.

Traditional orchid harvesting did not threaten the wild tubers, but now they are becoming scarcer. Ten years ago, said one collector, he had to walk for 30 minutes to reach the rich harvesting areas, but now it could take five hours. One current focus of orchid tuber harvesting is the Kitulo Plateau.

Satyrium

Income supplements are large for the local people when compared to the money they get for cash crops and farming. Intervention to manage the trade could affect their livelihoods and thus any action must be appropriate and sensitive. It is envisaged that tourism will provide an alternative, lucrative and more sustainable source of revenue for the local people.

To get to Kitulo, the best way for the visitor is to turn south off the main tarred road connecting Tanzania and Zambia at Chimala, about an hour's drive from Mbeya. Then travel up the escarpment through Matamba. The Tukuyu road connection has recently been repaired and offers an alternative route up the plateau from the west.

Camping on the Kitulo Plateau is the best option. The nearest place for the visitor to stay is at a small hostel at Makamba but this rarely has any electricity and no e-mail. There are also local hotels on the main road at Chimala two hours away or in Tukuyu to the south.

The Kitulo Plateau consists of 273 sq km of Afromontane and Afroalpine grassland and the area has long been heralded as a botanist's paradise containing many regional endemic flowering plants including the now threatened terrestrial orchids.

Perched above 2,600 metres between the Kipengere Range and the Uporoto and Livingstone mountains, Kitulo is the largest and most important plateau grassland in Tanzania today.

During the long dry season from May to November, temperatures drop, often to below freezing, and frosts are not uncommon. The onset of the rains drifting up from Lake Nyasa in November, however, brings a dramatic change to the plateau.

The landscape is transformed by the abundance of flowering plants blooming in succession and this has long drawn botanists and other visitors from around the world. The plateau contains 45 species of orchids of which 16 are endemic to the region.

Purple flowers of a Sylvatica

The area is also the home of important animal species including national and regional endemics, while breeding colonies of Blue swallow, Denham's bustard, Lesser kestrel, Pallid harrier, Njombe cisticola and Kipengere seedeater has brought the classification of an Important Bird Area (IBA) to Kitulo.

Other interesting fauna include the Ukinga montane skink and the Ukinga hornless chameleon, both restricted to montane grasslands in Tanzania's Southern Highlands. Meanwhile, the beautiful and aptly named Variable reed frog is common on the plateau, while one of Tanzania's rarest butterflies, *Neocoenyra petersi* may be seen in January and February.

Neocoenyra petersi on a leaf

The Southern Highlands Conservation Programme (SHCP), the Wildlife Conservation Society of Tanzania and Tanzania National Parks encouraged the granting of greater protection to this unique site and this was partially met in February 2002 when the Tanzanian government announced that 402 sq km of Kitulo would become a national park.

The challenge now is to establish a management system that takes into account the needs of the surrounding communities as well as giving Kitulo its status as a unique botanical area.

Apart from the Kitulo Plateau, the Southern Highlands of Tanzania includes Mount Rungwe, Uporoto, Ngosi, Ukinga, the Mbeya Range, the Livingstone Mountains, Umalila and the Ufipa Plateau.

Mount Rungwe is a dormant 2,960-metre volcano rising above the small town of Tukuyu that lies to the southeast of Mbeya. This cone was formed 2.5 million years ago, and the volcano marks the junction of the eastern and western arms of Africa's Great Rift Valley.

It is noted as an important centre of endemism and the mountain represents the pivot between the three great montane regions of eastern, central and southern Africa. The mountain's unbroken forest from 1,500 to 2,300 metres is of particular significance and wildlife includes the threatened Abbot's duiker.

View of Kitulo plateau with threatening clouds behind the mountains

Its importance also lies in the water it catches and distributes. Mount Rungwe's forest provide the water for the towns of Kiwira and Tukuyu as well as the fertile Kyela Valley while the important rivers of the area feed into Lake Nyasa.

Just a few miles northwest of Rungwe off the main Uyole to Tukuyu road at Mbete 1, one can visit the Ngosi Crater Lake within the 90 sq km Mporoto Forest Reserve. An hour's climb through bamboo and montane forest is rewarded with a spectacular view down inside the crater to the lake below.

Ngosi means "big" in the local Kisafwa language. Rising to 2,620 metres above sea level, Ngosi is the highest point within the reserve. The crater boasts 300 metre high, vertical walls providing a stunning backdrop to the emerald green water below. Some 2.6 km across, 4 sq km in area and at least 75 metres deep, Ngosi is the largest lake of its kind in the area.

The Ufipa Plateau in the Rukwa Region of Sumbawanga District is also worth visiting, while a little further on is the Katavi National Park with its dense concentration of wildlife including buffalo and hippopotamus.

This plateau sits high on the escarpment above the Lake Rukwa Valley and its mosaic of high forest and montane grassland represents the crossroads of four distinct ecological regions.

The Mbisi Forest Reserve is the eastern-most portion of Congolian forest in Tanzania and it is here that the Central African Red colobus monkey may be seen. Due to the high altitude and resulting lower temperatures, this population has grown longer coats than those found elsewhere in Africa.

Kniphofia

Much of southern Tanzania used to be referred to as "the forgotten south". But today, partially as a result of the work of the Southern Highlands Conservation Programme, the south of the country, with its magnificent scenery and unique flora and fauna, is gaining greater attention.

MIKUMI NATIONAL PARK

Some years ago, close to the house of the chief warden of Mikumi, a male elephant was drinking from a water tap he had just turned on. An empty bottle of Tusker beer stood on a table nearby and my wife was seated at the table. A nice composite picture I thought.

So intent was I on focusing that I did not realize my wife had hurriedly left her chair and that stones were hurtling over my shoulder in an attempt to distract the elephant that was charging at me. When I recognized what was happening, I also fled.

Visitors photographing elephants at Mikumi

Years later I got rather too close to the Mikumi hippopotamus pool when the dominant male charged me. He was in a grumpy mood, his back being badly sunburned by the drop in water level due to the drought. And he was only protecting his family.

Again, I was so focused on the camera that I did not see what was happening. This time there were no stones; the driver/guide with me had wisely headed for safety. The hippopotamus was either faking his charge or was simply taken aback by a person continuing to take pictures oblivious to the imminent danger.

Opposite page: Maasai giraffe

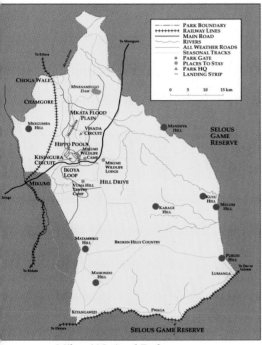

Mikumi National Park

One lesson clearly emerges from these incidents: never take wild animals lightly for all are dangerous. Elephants can turn vehicles over and hippopotamuses, it is said, kill more people than any other animal in Africa.

Mikumi is the access point for the southern Tanzania tourist circuit. The Selous Game Reserve abuts onto the southern section of Mikumi National Park while two hours to the southwest lies Udzungwa. Ruaha, located near the town of Iringa, is a further four hours from Mikumi and beyond is the orchid-rich Kitulo Plateau. Less than three hours away over a good tarmac road is Dar es Salaam.

Most people who visit Mikumi see only 15 percent of the park that lies north of the Dar es Salaam-to-Iringa road. This area is known as the Mkata Flood Plain and is notable for its fine-particle, clay-based, black cotton soil, named after the type of soil where cotton thrives.

During the rainy season, the black cotton soil is transformed into clogging mud, making some of this area inaccessible to vehicles. Nevertheless, this is the only developed area of Mikumi National Park and even during the rains the visitors are likely to see herds of elephants, lions (most frequently found on the Mkata Flood Plain), giraffes, skittish wildebeest, zebras, warthogs, shy elands and herds of buffalo and impala.

Brief profile

Declared in August 1964, Mikumi is Tanzania's fourth largest park
After two additions, the park is now 3,230 sq km in size
To the south 1,968 sq km was added so Mikumi now joins the Selous
In the north 162 sq km was added north of the Mkata River
Malundwe Hill at 1,257 metres is the park's highest point
Mikumi was a Game Controlled Area from 1954 to protect it from hunters
Outside the park, subsistence farmers grow maize, sorghum and cassava
Only the northern 15 percent of the park is usually visited
The best months are in the dry season from June to November
In the wet season part of the northern section is impassable due to mud
At least 32 large mammal species, including elephants, have been seen
Others include lion, giraffe, buffalo, hippopotamus, zebra, wildebeest,
impala, eland, hunting dog, kudu, sable, yellow baboon and jackal.

Of all the Tanzanian parks, Mikumi is the most visited. But most of the visitors simply pass through the park by train, bus, truck or car without paying any entry fees to Mikumi.

Two railways, a road, power lines and the oil pipeline to Zambia in the southwest, dissect the park. Given the amount of traffic, wild animals are inevitably killed on the rail and the road despite the warning signs and the speed humps along the main road.

English and Swahili signs warn of the dangers ahead.

For Dar es Salaam residents, Mikumi is the nearest escape and with the tarred road and improved accommodation, they are coming in increasing numbers.

A tented camp lies to the south of the main road at Vuma Hill and there is another camp just north of the road. Mikumi also has a youth hostel and campsites, and there are a number of hotels and guesthouses in Mikumi town just outside the park.

One of the roads from Vuma Hill cuts through ravined and forested country for some three hours before joining the Tanzania-Zambia (TAZARA) railway on the boundary that connects to the northern section of the Selous.

It is planned to make this into an all-weather road that follows the ridges, thereby avoiding rivers and the need to build bridges. Such ridges have been used since time immemorial by the elephants and other wildlife that prefer to keep their feet dry.

Giraffe

The giraffe is Tanzania's national animal and is protected throughout the country. The giraffe (twiga in Swahili) figures in the names of many companies and on many logos.

The rosette-type patches of a Maasai giraffe (above right) distinguish it from the reticulated giraffe shown at left.

The visitor to Tanzania will see Maasai giraffe. In other countries further south, Reticulated giraffe are encountered. The shape of their respective patches helps the visitor to identify which of the two sub-species they are seeing.

Scientifically, giraffe are called Giraffa camelopadalis that appears to derive from an Arabic word xirapha meaning "one who walks swiftly". Camelopadalis refers to their size and markings and means, "as big as a camel" and "spotted like a leopard".

Trees and other plants distinguish Mikumi. Marula trees (*Mng'ongo* in Swahili) are common. This tree occurs in deciduous, wooded grassland from South Africa to Ethiopia and the fruit is used to make the Amarula Wild Fruit Cream drink that is indigenous to Africa.

The tree grows up to 15 metres in height, has a thick trunk and long branches. The crown is round, the bark grey to black and the leaves are crowded at the end of the branches. The flowers are pale green to greeny-pink and the fruit is plum-shaped and tastes like a mango.

Borassus palms from which the name Mikumi is derived, and Marula fruit (right)

Elephants regard the Marula as a delicacy, vigorously shaking the tree to dislodge the fruit. In South Africa, where Amarula Wild Fruit Cream is produced, the marula is known as the "elephant tree" although it is not true that elephants get drunk on the fruit.

Tamarind with its many medicinal uses, grotesque but distinctive baobabs, sausage, cassia, black thorn and African blackwood trees exist at Mikumi as do a profusion of flowers alongside the main road at certain times of the year.

Village names

The naming of a village after the dominant tree in an area is common in east Africa. Many villages are called mbuyuni. Mbuyu is the Swahili word for the baobab tree and the ending of the word on "ni" simply means "of" or "at" the baobab tree.

Another village, Mgoza, is so-named in the Wavindunda dialect as denoting the African star-chestnut tree while a third is called Ikoya meaning a Cape fig tree in the local dialect.

Mikumi village was established in 1914 by the Wavindunda people. Its name is taken from the local word *mikuky* used in their dialect for the borassus palm. These trees grew in profusion around the village and were used by the original inhabitants to build and thatch houses and to make a local brew.

Mikumi has two distinct geological formations that, with some variations, are found north and west on the Mkata Flood Plain, and to the south in the area abutting the Selous. Vegetation, animals and birdlife may vary greatly between these two areas.

View from Vuma Hill across the road that dissects the park with Mkata Flood Plain beyond

African buffalo

The park lies in a horseshoe of mountains and hills. Precambrian 600-million-year-old rocks underlie the hills while the Mkata Flood Plain is primarily flat and composed of alluvium soils that are alkaline and sodium. The Precambrian rocks that form the hills are part of the Dodoma system of central Tanzania.

The wild animals in the southern section of Mikumi National Park are unused to vehicles and tourists and tend to run away at the slightest disturbance. During the poaching scourge of the 1970s and 1980s, this was an unprotected area for animals (particularly elephants) migrating from the Selous to Mikumi.

It will take some time to win back the animals' confidence and to convince them that a vehicle and visitors equipped with cameras are different to those with guns who came before. But such confidence is gradually returning.

Lioness

RUAHA NATIONAL PARK

In terms of its size, remoteness, wilderness quality, austere baobab trees, large concentrations of rare species and few visitors, Ruaha is unrivalled. It is located 130 km from the town of Iringa and 625 km southwest of Dar es Salaam towards Zambia.

Brief profile

Ruaha was declared a national park in 1964
With a small addition in 1974, it is 10,300 sq km
It is the second largest park after Serengeti
Ruaha is a linguistic corruption of "luvaha"
This word in Hehe means river, brook or stream
456 birds and 1,600 plant species identified
50 species of amphibians/reptiles have been seen
The park (1) is in a larger ecosystem of protected areas.

A most memorable sighting at Ruaha is of a mature, spiral-horned male greater kudu. Greater kudu males are solitary or found in bachelor herds except during mating. In contrast, females may be seen throughout the year, usually in dense bush country in groups of 6 to 10 including their offspring.

The cryptic colouring of kudu, plus the fact that they stand still when alarmed, means that they blend into the bush and the visitor may drive up to one without even seeing it.

Female greater kudu

Opposite page: Greater kudu

To the untrained eye, greater and lesser kudu may look similar. But as a guideline: lesser kudu are smaller in size with smaller horns, they have two conspicuous white patches on the upper and lower neck and about 6 lateral white stripes on their bodies compared to 11-15 stripes on the greater kudu.

Giraffe framed by a baobab tree

Kudu look and move with great elegance and walk hesitantly when approaching water. The horns of male greater kudu can reach 180 cm in a series of graceful spirals. But they are rarely used for fighting or defense against predators.

In wooded country, the kudu tilts its chin skywards with horns along its back to avoid becoming tangled in the thicket. The horns are greatly prized in African countries as musical instruments, containers for honey and ritual objects.

Elephants are in abundance and Ruaha has been nicknamed "Giraffic Park" because of its 8,000 Maasai giraffe.

Another animal found at Ruaha is the African hunting dog. These elusive and enigmatic animals are relatively common in Ruaha but are threatened with extinction in most places in Africa by motorists, hunters and canine fever from which they have no immunity.

Once they were known as "wild dogs" and classified as "vermin" by the colonial authorities because it was said they drove wildlife out of an area and threatened domestic stock. A price was put on their heads and they were randomly shot.

Lycaon pictus, as they are known scientifically, literally translates as "painted wolf". But even this is a misnomer for this dog-like animal with rounded ears, a blotched mustard, black and white coat and white-tipped tail, behaves passively.

For nine months a year, they hunt at a fast, loping pace covering hundreds of sq km. The remainder of the year is spent mating, close to their new litter or caring lovingly for other pups. They are very sociable animals, continually greeting each other and noisily anticipating their next meal.

African hunting dogs

Sable antelope are related to the roan antelope and both species exist at Ruaha. Male sables are magnificent animals with glossy black coats, mainly white faces and scimitar horns. Females have smaller horns and chestnut-brown coats. The offspring are born with a paler coloured coat.

Sable can often be seen in *miombo* (*Brachystigia*) woodland along Ruaha's Mpululu road starting at the sand river at Mwagusi, where there is an excellent tented camp. Male sable are solitary while females and young are usually found in family groups.

Roan antelope may also be seen. They are rusty-grey in colour, have large fringed ears, black and white facial marking and boldly ridged, backward sweeping horns. Those worn by the males are considerably thicker and more curved than those of the females.

Roan will canter away before stopping to look at the intruder. They are mainly grazers feeding on leaves but they may browse on tender twigs. They drink regularly, usually in the morning. They are usually seen in the thick *acacia* groves near the park headquarters.

The Great Ruaha River

You may also see eland, the largest antelope weighing up to 800 kg, hartebeest (called *kongoni* in Swahili), Grant's gazelle (on the southern limit of their distribution), Defassa waterbuck, Kirk's dik-dik, Bushbuck, Bohor reedbuck and Maasai klipspringer on the rocks.

Lying in the rain shadow of the Udzungwa Mountains, the park is bisected by the Great Ruaha River. It is the most southern extension of the Maasai Steppes and is among the most arid of Tanzania's 14 national parks.

The proximity of the Udzungwa Mountains is important for they act as a formidable obstacle to the inward flow of rain clouds from the Indian Ocean. The clouds break up on the mountains and Ruaha receives the overspill from Udzungwa.

The base rock of Ruaha is probably 450 to 600 million years old. Upward faulting of the earth's crust resulted in buckling that created the mountains. Downward faulting created the Great Rift Valley of which the Great Ruaha River is an extension.

Recently, the reduced amount of water flowing along the river has concerned Tanzanian electricity consumers as well as conservationists. Rice schemes upstream are thought to have affected the flow to the downstream Mtera and Kidatu dams that were constructed to supply electricity to 75 percent of Tanzania's people.

Climate

The short rains (vuli in Swahili) should fall in October and November; the long rains (masika in Swahili) from January to May. In February there should be a lull for "cleaning up". This cycle is known as "single season rains".

Rainfall in Ruaha National Park averages around 500 mm in the valley to 800 mm on the escarpment. Just before the rains, maximum daytime temperatures can rise to 40 degrees C dropping to 25 degrees C at night. During the cooler June/July months, the daytime temperature drops to 30 degrees C and 15 degrees C at night.

For avid bird watchers and butterfly collectors, the best months at Ruaha are January to May. For other visitors, the best months are in the cool season from May to November. In October and November as it gets warmer, spectacular lightning and thunderstorms occur.

A plateau, that is about 100 metres higher to the northeast, dominates the park. Most people visit the 20 percent of the park along the Great Ruaha River because of its better-developed road network, accommodation and game viewing opportunities.

Much of Ruaha National Park was once the home of the Wahehe people who still dominate in Iringa and the surrounding area. Before their arrival, scattered groups of hunter-gatherers known by anthropologists as Kosi Samba, resided in the area.

Under the formidable Chief Mkwawa, the Wahehe spearheaded local African resistance to German colonialism at the end of the 19th century. Their chilling war cry of *"hee-hee"* once reverberated through the granite *kopjes* (rock outcrops) that today's visitor will see before reaching Iringa town.

The Wahehe killed a 10-man German patrol near Iringa and a price was placed on Chief Mkwawa's head. The chief finally committed suicide rather than be captured and his head was displayed in the Bremen Anthropological Museum until l964.

Then it was returned to his grandson, Chief Adam Sapi, the speaker of independent Tanzania's first parliament. The skull was buried in the family cemetery near Ruaha.

Another monument to the country's rich history is found at Isimila, 20 km south of Iringa on the Mbeya road. Isimila dates back some 60,000 years and contains Stone Age tools, weapons and dramatic sandstone columns that stand as mute sentinels to a bygone era.

The stark sandstone columns at Isimila

Ruaha is a transition zone where much of the flora and fauna that distinguishes east and southern Africa meets and overlaps. Being able to see greater and lesser kudu, sable and roan in one park is part of Ruaha's special attraction. And this is also the southern limit of the Grant's gazelle.

There are also lions, leopards, cheetahs, African hunting dogs, innumerable elephants, a good percentage of which are tuskless, and giraffes. There is also abundant plains game such as zebra and impala while hippopotamus clamber from the water in broad daylight. Old male buffaloes graze around the park headquarters.

Hippopotamus changing pools in the Great Ruaha River

Ruaha's ecosystem covers some 40,000 sq km embracing several neighbouring game reserves and the park contains four main vegetation zones. Acacia is found in the extreme east, to the southwest there is *miombo* and *commiphora* is found in the southwest where there are also small pockets of *drypetes*.

The birdlife is spectacular as evidenced by the 456 species so far identified. The park is noted for its significant number of rare migrant Eleanor's falcons that may be seen in December/January and new species await discovery.

The solitude and sheer breathtaking beauty make Ruaha the Africa of the imagination, with very few tourists and even fewer cars.

SELOUS GAME RESERVE

The Selous (pronounced without the last "s") is known in Swahili as *Shamba la Bibi* that literally translated means "women's garden". It is 48,000 sq km covering almost six percent of Tanzania's land surface -- larger than Switzerland or the American states of New Hampshire and New Jersey.

It has the largest number of several species of animals found in a single reserve anywhere in the world: elephant (65,000), buffalo (110,000), hippopotamus (40,000), lion (over 3,000) and the endangered African hunting dog (1,300).

Over 440 species of birds have been identified in the Selous, which is a pristine wilderness area with only a few photographic visitors a year.

Arusha Manifesto

Back in September 1961, on the eve of the country's independence, Tanzania's first president, Julius Nyerere, said in a speech known as the Arusha Manifesto:

"In accepting the trusteeship of our wildlife, we solemnly declare that we will do everything in our power to make sure that our children's grandchildren will be able to enjoy this rich and precious inheritance.

"The conservation of wildlife and wild places calls for specialist knowledge, trained manpower, and money and we look to other nations to cooperate with us in this important task -- the success or failure of which not only affects the continent of Africa but the rest of the world as well."

Specialist knowledge and trained personnel now exist. But each anti-poaching game scout has to cover 140 sq km, an area almost the size of the District of Columbia in the USA that is covered by the Washington DC police force and other agencies.

The money that Nyerere sought in 1961 has not been forthcoming. The USA and Switzerland, despite their being vastly richer, spend less per capita per annum on conservation that do more than the 30 millionTanzanians.

Opposite page: The Selous contains about half of the African hunting dogs left in the world.

Some 400 foreign hunters visit the Selous annually. In the 1960s they demanded a "hundred-pounder" as an elephant with that weight of tusks on either side was known. Today, largely because of poachers, there are few with tusks of more than 80 lbs a side.

Male sable

In the dry season from July to November, the hunters are in assigned "blocks" shooting some 3,000 animals while generating 80 percent of the reserve's annual income of over US$3 million. The 6,000 photographic tourists vastly exceed the number of hunters but they generate only 20 percent of the reserve's income.

Game hunting is a harsh economic reality. Tanzania must generate income to support its conservation efforts and it is forced to attract hunters and tourists, who visit different areas.

Black rhinoceros

In September 1973, ignited by the anti-hunting lobby, the government of Tanzania imposed a ban throughout the country. This ban lasted until 1982. The income from big game hunting disappeared and this had a disastrous affect on the Selous. One result was the commercial poaching of the 1970s and 1980s.

A 1976 aerial count estimated the number of elephants in the Selous at 110,000. As a result of poaching, this figure was said to have fallen to under 30,000 by 1991. In the early 1980s, the black rhinoceros population in the Selous was decimated from its estimated 3,000, then the largest population of any group in Africa. Today both are showing signs of recovery.

The number of elephants, it must be stressed, is only an estimate. In northern Mozambique's Niassa Game Reserve south of the Selous, 11,000 elephants were recently "found". That a six-tonne animal can be "found" defies normal logic. Yet I was given an explanation in Mozambique. During the war there the elephants simply "disappeared" in search of safer pastures. They only "reappeared" once the war was over. Furthermore, because the area was at war, the likelihood of outsiders seeing or counting the elephants was greatly diminished.

The Selous ecosystem encompasses a wide spectrum of wildlife habitats including open grasslands, *miombo* woodlands that cover three-quarters of the reserve, and riverine forests. As a result of its unique ecological importance, the Selous was declared a World Heritage Site in 1982.

Elephants silhouetted by dust and the sunset

The northern sector, where high-paying visitors are encouraged, contains all three types of habitat. Open grassland supports such species as wildebeest and zebra. In the *miombo* woodlands draping the mountains and ridges around Beho Beho and Stiegler's Gorge, the visitor may see Greater kudu and Roosevelt's sable. In the riverine thickets with their plentiful Borassus palms, elephants, hippopotamus, antelope and crocodiles are found.

Leopard hunting hyrax in Stiegler's Gorge

The birdlife of the Selous is spectacular. The ever-changing course of the Rufiji River with its many sandbanks, lakes, lagoons and islands draws many waterbirds. A safari by riverboat is highly recommended. So, too are the walking safaris and longer trekking.

The bird specialist may see the White-headed lapwing along the Rufiji River and the rare White-collared pratincole on fast flowing sections of the river. Pels fishing owls are more likely to be heard at night than seen and the White-backed night heron is another elusive, nocturnal species.

Racquet-tailed rollers are to be found outside the *miombo* country and Thick-billed cuckoo may be seen flying over the treetops. Rare Red-necked falcon may be found close to Borassus palms and the keen-sighted Bateleur eagles often direct vultures to carcasses.

Diminutive Malachite kingfisher

The untidy grass nests the visitor may see are probably those of the abundant White-browed sparrow weavers. The Selous is the stronghold of Livingstone's flycatcher while the Dark-backed weaver is conspicuous over drainage lines.

Much of the northern Selous is set aside for photographic tourism. This area contains the greatest numbers of wildlife and is the most beautiful part of the ecosystem. To the north lies the TAZARA (Tanzania to Zambia) railway that runs along the southern boundary of Mikumi National Park.

To the east is the reserve's boundary, to the west Steigler's Gorge (named after a Swiss adventurer who was killed by an elephant in about 1900) and the road to the headquarters at Matambwe, while to the south is the Rufiji River. For the moment, the areas to the south of the Rufiji and Ruaha rivers are undeveloped.

Outside the Selous in the Rufiji Delta is the final resting place of the German light cruiser, the *Konigsberg* that was sunk by the British Royal Navy in the First World War. The guns were removed from the cruiser and hauled overland playing a considerable role in the East Africa campaign.

One of the many Nile crocodiles in the Rufiji River

View of the Rifiji River

In this war, armies traversed the Selous and there are still traces of this action today. Trenches, spent cartridge cases and the rehabilitated grave of Frederick Courtenay Selous, after whom the British named the reserve, bear mute testimony to a bygone era.

Selous was the son of a chairman of the London Stock Exchange. Born in England in 1851, he became a noted naturalist, conservationist and big game hunter. He was killed in 1917 while a Captain leading a detachment of the 25th Royal Fusiliers against a German position near Beho Beho.

The German sniper who shot Selous was part of the vastly outnumbered force led by General Paul von Lettow Vorbeck to defend *Deutsch Ost-Afrika* (then the German colony that is today Tanzania) from the Allied forces. Vorbeck used guerrilla tactics throughout the war and only surrendered after the 1918 armistice.

Visitors are constantly irritated by tsetse flies in wildlife areas. But the tsetse flies are the greatest allies of wild animals, keeping humans and domestic livestock at bay.

Using the potency of the tsetse, the British colonial administration that inherited the country from the Germans moved the African people away from their scattered hamlets in the Selous, into villages where schools and health services were made available.

This forced migration from the Selous became known in Swahili as the *kihamo* (or simply "migration" in English) to which old people still refer with disgust. Traditional homes, smallholdings and the culturally important burial places of previous generations were abandoned as people were moved outside the Selous to settle.

Eccentrics

Ionides

English eccentrics were common in the Selous and surrounding area in the 1960s. Latham Leslie-Moore occupied a small strip of land that became an island only at high tide. He refused to recognize Tanzania's independence in December 1961, petitioning the United Nations for the separate independence of his "island" home that he called Whispering Palms.

The biggest eccentric of them all was an Englishman with the unlikely name of Constantine Ionides. He was responsible for elephant control in an area covering thousands of sq km including much of the contemporary Selous. But he was better known internationally as one of the world's top snake-catchers and a book was written about him called Snake Man.

Ionides, or "Iodine" to his friends, and known to Africans as kibuko (Swahili for the hippopotamus-hide whip he used on poachers and others), was said to have been sitting in the dark in his long-drop toilet outside when a snake crawled over his legs. He identified the snake and ran inside for his stick, catching a huge Black mamba.

Another story was that the rafters of his house were filled with snakes and if a guest flinched when one fell into their soup or some such dish, Ionides would order them out. These, and many other European eccentrics, were my introduction to southern Tanzania.

UDZUNGWA MOUNTAINS
NATIONAL PARK

When the APG area-specific guide to Udzungwa Mountains National Park was first published in late 1999, the best known bookshop in Dar es Salaam decided not to put the book on public sale until the following year.

The owner of the bookshop, her husband and two friends planned to spend the millennium camping close to the 170-metre Sanje waterfall in Udzungwa and they did not want their holiday disrupted by other visitors

Climber limits and increased fees had not deterred bookings for the visitors to see in the new millennium from Africa's summit, Mount Kilimanjaro. So the less well known Udzungwa Mountains remained one of few places where the visitor was guaranteed privacy.

Brief profile

Declared on 29 February 1992 and known as UMNP
Total area of the Udzungwa Mountains is 10,000 sq km
UMNP is 1,990 sq km and contains many endemic species
The park is located 370 km southwest of Dar es Salaam
Highest peak is Luhomero, 2,576 metres above sea level
Rainfall is 2,000 mm (80 inches) a year in the southeast
On the western side the annual rainfall drops to 600 mm
Visitors need warm clothing from May to August and…
Raincoats from October to May during the wet season
Best time to visit is in the June to October dry season
Trails may be slippery during the remainder of the year.

A violet on the forest floor

Udzungwa Mountains National Park has no tourist accommodation. It is a camping and hiking wilderness retreat with few defined trails, extremely beautiful scenery including endemic trees, shrubs and herbs, and precious few visitors.

Opposite page: Sanje waterfall

It also reflects the interests of and compromises made by environmentalists and the local people. Centuries old traditions were recognized when the park was created. The local people still collect leaves, bark and roots that, along with trees, shrubs and herbs, are used for traditional medicine.

In the late 1990s, Udzungwa averaged only one visitor a day. Now the number has more than tripled and is still climbing. While Udzungwa is not as well known as Serengeti, Ngorongoro and Kilimanjaro, it was the fourth guidebook that TANAPA reprinted.

Udzungwa is part of the Eastern Arc of mountains that Tanzania. Known as the "Galapagos of Africa", the arc begins to the north in Kenya. But most of the arc is in Tanzania and includes the Pare, Usambara, Uluguru and Mahenge mountains.

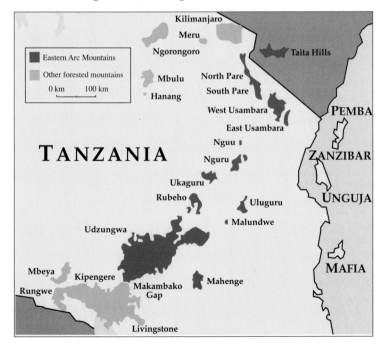

The arc comprises of 11 main geologically separated blocks of mountains that contain a patchwork of diminishing dense tropical forest that is notable for its high rainfall.

The eastern arc tropical forests are about 30 million years old, the rock at their base probably 450 to 600 million years old. Udzungwa Mountains rose from the land surface as a result of upward faulting in the earth's crust resulting in buckling and uplifting.

The mountains were formed by a fusion of the ancient Mozambique shield and Archaean granites. Weathering and erosion then shaped the present geological boundary roughly along the central watershed.

The mountain range of the arc makes up only two percent of Tanzania's land area, but the forests contain 30 to 40 percent of the country's plant and mammal species. They also have the second highest bird diversity in Africa behind the less accessible Ituri Forest in the Democratic Republic of Congo (DRC).

Conditions range from humid to temperate and this, coupled with the moist cloak of evergreen forests that have been ecologically stable for thousands of years, makes Udzungwa an important birding area where 250 species have been identified to date.

The Eastern Arc is the core area for 25 or so bird species that exist only in Tanzania with Udzungwa possessing about half of these.

Painting of Udzungwa forest partridges

One of the most recent avian finds has been the Udzungwa forest partridge that is classified as "globally threatened".

Udzungwa contains far higher densities of specific rare birds than occur elsewhere. These include the Dappled mountain robin, White-chested alethe, Sharp's akalat, the Olive-flanked ground robin, Spot-throat, Black-backed cisticola and the Red-capped forest warbler.

Swynnerton's robin, once believed to be confined to eastern Zimbabwe is now known to exist in abundance at Udzungwa. When the Rufous-winged sunbird was identified at Udzungwa in 1981, its sighting was regarded as a major event in Afrotropical ornithology.

Roughly 20 percent of Udzungwa is closed canopy forest. The remainder is divided between woodland, grassland and dry Somali/Maasai arid woodland in the extreme northeast of the park along the Great Ruaha River where young baobab trees grow.

Udzungwa has elephant, buffalo, lion and leopard on the plateau. But, apart from the inaccessibility of the plateau and the camouflage these animals find, these species will be seen more easily at Mikumi National Park only two hours away.

What sets Udzungwa apart is its scenery and smaller mammals such as primates, antelopes and bushbabies (known as galagos by scientists), amphibians and reptiles.

Both the Sanje crested mangabey and the Iringa red colobus monkey, endemic to Udzungwa and classified as endangered, as well as the Tanzanian black-and-white colobus, Sykes and Vervet monkeys, and the Yellow baboon, may all be seen.

In 1979, the Sanje crested mangabey was first identified in Udzungwa by two wildlife ecology lecturers from Dar es Salaam University. It was isolated from the next known population by 1,000 km (600 miles).

A tame Sanje crested mangabey (locally known as *n'golaga*) was in a nearby village. Named Tulia (meaning "calm down" in Swahili), this mangabey was transported to Arusha where it lived until 2002.

Tulia at six months of age

Black-and-white colobus and Sykes monkeys are visible in the light foliage along the roadside and Yellow baboons wreak havoc with villagers' crops thereby causing considerable anger.

Black-and-white colobus changes trees

Bushbabies feed at night on insects, tree gum and fruit, when there is less competition from monkeys and baboons. They are very attractive, furry creatures with large eyes and ears. Their loud call is reminiscent of the cackle of a francolin.

Two species, the Matundu dwarf galago and the Mountain dwarf galago, have so far been identified at Udzungwa. A third species, the Greater galago, almost certainly exists and like the Udzungwa forest partridge and Sanje crested mangabey, it too is waiting to be "discovered".

Bearded pygmy chameleon slowly adances

Amphibians and reptiles abound at Udzungwa. Chameleons are known as "slow foot" because of their ponderous and deliberate gait. In Africa you will see few, and then usually when they are crossing the road. But in Udzungwa several members of this family exist such as the Spiny-sided, Tubercle-nosed, Tanzania goetze, Werner's three-horned, the One-horned and the Flap-necked.

Bearded-pygmy chameleons with their short, prehensile tails change colour less than other chameleons. They may be seen on vegetation beside forest trails.

Chameleons are related to lizards and there are no poisonous species in Africa. Apart from the Indian Ocean island of Madagascar, Tanzania has the highest number of chameleons found in the world. They can play a very useful role; instead of conventional flypaper, chameleons on windowsills can devour incoming insects!

Frogs and toads also exist in abundance. Some, like the brightly coloured tree frogs, change their colour to avoid detection. The large Uluguru tree frogs are a delicate light green, sometimes with yellow patterning resembling a small patch of fungus, making them very hard to see.

The nocturnal Parker's tree frog has rusty red to orange eyes that you may pick out at night with a torch by following its clacking call. Leaf litter frogs and bush squeakers are more likely to be heard than seen.

Udzungwa puddle frogs, first scientifically described in 1983, are tiny with a distinct light band across the top of their heads between the eyes. Above 1,200 metres there are the "sticky" frogs that produce a mucous that is not harmful but should be kept away from cuts, scratches, the eyes, ears, nose and lips where they may cause irritation.

Montane torrent frog

In the rainy season between November and May, Udzungwa is a very good place for aesthetically beautiful butterflies. Dietary preferences vary greatly and awareness of this will lead you to their preferred habitat where you can observe butterflies' personal habits.

Of Africa's 3,000 plus species of butterflies, 1,370 exist in Tanzania, the largest figure in any East African country. Of these, 121 are found only in Tanzania. Just how many exist in the Udzungwa Mountains is presently unknown and this is another under-researched field. Certainly two or three species are endemic to the Udzungwa Mountains.

Several species of swallowtails will be found in the Sanje Falls area. Forty species have been recorded in Tanzania, that is roughly half of those found in Africa's Afrotropical region. One particular swallowtail to watch for in the Sanje area is the Horniman swallowtail, a small group of which only a male has been captured so far.

GOMBE NATIONAL PARK

Gombe Stream, internationally renowned for its chimpanzees, is Tanzania's smallest national park. It lies 16 km north of Kigoma, the regional capital, and adjoins Lake Tanganyika which was formed 10 million years ago and is the world's second deepest lake.

Gombe is a little over 16 km in length and 3 km at its widest point. It is a narrow strip of montane forest cut by steep-sided valleys that are gauged into the landscape by swift flowing mountain steams. Around it is cleared, agricultural land.

The park lies on the western arm of the Great Rift Valley, a 6,500 km crack in the earth's crust that was caused by the eastward drift of the rest of the continent. The trough left by this upheaval was filled by Lake Tanganyika, the bottom of which is 1,470 metres below sea level.

Brief profile

Gombe Stream was gazetted on 21 June 1968
Previously it had been a game reserve
The park covers only 52 sq km (20 sq miles)
The dry season months are best for visitors
Chimpanzees are the focus of any visit but...
Red colobus, red-tailed and other monkeys may be seen
There are also leopards, bushpigs and bushbucks
Waterfalls and evergreen forests are found
The area has a rich history from early Africans to
Slavers and British explorers like Livingstone.

The lake drains rivers in Burundi, Tanzania, Democratic Republic of Congo and Zambia. The lake level does not vary in height by more than one metre despite the large rivers flowing into it. Sand, shingle and rocks litter the foreshore.

The underlying rock at Gombe, as in most of Africa, is ancient gneiss with underlying quartzites on the upper slopes. In some places, younger sandstones have faulted downwards producing the red cliffs. The lake is notable for its sunsets.

Opposite page: Flo had ragged ears, a deformed nose and worn down teeth. But when she died of old age on 22 August 1972, her passing was marked by an obituary in a reputable London newspaper, the first one for a chimpanzee.

Gombe with Lake Tanganyika beyond

Jane Goodall, the human "mother" of Gombe's chimpanzees looking for them

Approximately 120 chimpanzees live at Gombe in three distinct territorial communities. In the north is the Mitumba group that has been studied for about 15 years. To the south is the Nyasanga group about which little is known.

The most studied community of chimpanzees is the Kasekela group in the centre of the park. Since research work began at Gombe in 1960, this group entered people's homes through the photographs and films of Hugo van Lawick and innumerable articles and books.

In 1960, paleontologist Louis Leakey of Olduvai Gorge fame sent a young British woman, Jane Goodall, to Gombe to study the chimpanzees to ascertain what could be learned about human evolution. Since then, Gombe has become the world's longest running study of wild animals.

At first, the shy and alert chimpanzees were unapproachable. But Goodall soon discovered that the chimpanzees liked fruit and bananas and by regularly feeding them from her Kasekela camp she persuaded them to overcome their fear of people.

Soon she could recognize individual chimpanzees and began documenting every aspect of their behaviour. Goodall began to describe their rich and varied social life and to discover that they shared many human traits including the making and use of tools, hunting and warfare.

At the beginning of the 19th century, there were an estimated 2 million chimpanzees in Africa. Now their number has shrunk to a maximum of 150,000 in small and fragmented communities.

Today, habitat destruction, disease, inbreeding, wars, humans hunting for food, medical research on captive chimpanzees, and zoos, all threaten the surviving population whom scientists have found to differ genetically from humans by just over 1 percent! Chimpanzees and humans share 98.6 percent of their genes.

Chimpanzees form friendships that can endure throughout their lives of 60 years or more. They swagger and punch, kiss and embrace. They have emotions such as happiness, anger, sadness and despair. They are capable of both brutality and compassion. The dividing line between chimpanzees and humans is indeed blurred.

Portrait of David Greybeard

It was one of the Gombe chimpanzees (named David Greybeard by Goodall), who in October 1960 first showed the British researcher that chimpanzees had mastered early tool-making, by stripping the leaves off a twig, poking it into a termite mound and eating the tasty insects.

David Greybeard, the first chimpanzee to explore the Kasekela camp, was also the first primate to be recorded using tool-making techniques and revealing that they are carnivores as well as vegetarians.

Flo using a fashioned twig to catch ants

Flo, at first sight the ugly matriarch of one of the families that Goodall found at Gombe, was the only chimpanzee to be honoured with an obituary in Britain's *Sunday Times* newspaper. The death of her son, Flint, close to the spot where Flo had died, makes heart-rending reading and taught Goodall about chimpanzees' capacity to grieve.

Gombe is also notable for its Red colobus and Red-tailed monkeys. The colobus are Central African red colobus and they are found in central Africa to the north and west of the Congo River, and in western Tanzania and Uganda.

Most have dark extremities of the hands and feet with red markings on the cap that tops the head. They are among the largest of the species of red colobus and tend to have thick coats to protect them against the climate of their mountain habitat.

The Red-tailed monkeys are very active with long red tails, dark blue faces and white or grizzled cheeks. They are found in eastern Congo, western parts of east Africa, the southern Sudan, Angola and northern Zambia. The colour of the nose spot denotes regional variation.

They make jerky movements of the head and forequarters and a very staccato, chirping alarm call that may be the first sign of their presence as well as a warning sound to other species in the area of intrusion.

The study of the baboons that are always present in the park began at Gombe Stream in 1966 and continues until this day.

People of this area belong to the Ha ethnic group. They are a very attractive Bantu people whose forebears reputedly moved into the Kigoma region surrounding the lake many centuries ago from West Africa. Others from Tanzania as well as refugees from Burundi and Congo have followed.

The Ha lived cushioned from the influence of the outside world until early in the 19th century when Arab traders from the coast travelled to Ujiji near Lake Tanganyika in search of slaves.

Ujiji became an infamous slave centre, as did the southwestern route to the area of Lake Nyasa. Zanzibar's current President, Amani Abeid Karume, traces his grandparents back to the Ujiji route.

Arab influence remains today in the Kigoma area. They brought the mango trees that grow in almost every village and the Muslim religion that marks the route through Tabora to the coast. They called Lake Tanganyika "Ujiji" after the town that was the base of their operations.

In the wake of the Arab slavers came the European explorers and missionaries. The most famous of these was David Livingstone while Richard Burton and John Hanning Speke were wrongly convinced that the source of the White Nile River lay in Lake Tanganyika.

Yoked slaves being driven to the coast

It was at Ujiji, just south of Kigoma, that the British-born American journalist Henry Morton Stanley, on assignment for his New York newspaper in 1871, found explorer David Livingstone who had disappeared from European sight five years earlier while exploring Lake Tanganyika. Today their meeting is marked by an unphotogenic monument.

Stanley, according to his own account, is reputed to have used the immortal words, "Dr Livingstone, I presume" to the Scottish explorer who had not seen a fellow European for years. Livingstone, with masterly English understatement, is said to have replied simply, "Yes?"

Burton and Speke had set out from the coast in search of the source of the White Nile. They followed the slavers' routes, reaching the lake in 1858. But Lake Tanganyika was too low to be the source of the White Nile. Furthermore it drains to the west and so could not be the source of the White Nile.

The exploration of such men was the prelude for the European "Scramble for Africa" during which the Germans laid claim to Tanganyika (the country became Tanzania in 1964 after the union between Tanganyika and Zanzibar), Rwanda and Burundi. It was during German colonial rule that the Dar es Salaam-to-Kigoma railway was built following the path trodden by the former Arab slavers.

The ship that went by train

The Germans built the 1,300 tonne Graf von Coetzen and shipped it by train to Kigoma where it was carefully assembled during the First World War. The ship was bombed before her maiden voyage and eventually sunk by the Germans as defeat in Europe became apparent.

Re-floated by the British in 1924, the ship was renamed the Liemba and starred in a film, The African Queen with Humphrey Bogart and Katherine Hepburn. Today the Liemba continues to carry passengers to the extremities of the lake.

The 1,250 km railway took nine years to complete and made Kigoma the major port of Lake Tanganyika. After the defeat of Germany in the First World War, Tanganyika became a British protectorate and Gombe Stream was designated as a game reserve in 1943 to protect the chimpanzees.

Today it no longer takes several days to reach Gombe. The visitor can fly to Kigoma and then take lake transport to the park, cutting the time to get there to a matter of hours. Kigoma has decent hotels and guesthouses and there is one tented camp in the park, as well as the park resthouse, *bandas* and a campsite.

View of the remaining dense forest at Gombe

Chimpanzees grooming each other

KATAVI NATIONAL PARK

Katavi Plains is noted for its spectacular dry season concentrations of big mammals, particularly buffalo, elephant, giraffe, eland, topi and zebra, the inevitable predators such as lion, leopard and hyena, as well as for its hippopotamus and African hunting dogs.

Except for Lake Manyara, the total number of animals per sq km in Katavi is higher than in any other protected area in East Africa, while densities of buffalo, roan, waterbuck and bushpig are higher than anywhere else in Tanzania. The areas around Lakes Chada and Katavi have the largest numbers of animals in the park.

Buffalo are the most numerous species followed by zebra, hippopotamus, waterbuck and impala. Densities of these animals vary according to the location and habitat.

Brief profile

Declared as a national park in 1974
Katavi was originally 1,823 sq km
In 1997 this was extended to 4,471 sq km
This made it Tanzania's third largest park
Only the Serengeti and Ruaha are bigger
June to October are the best visitor months.

Nowhere else other than at Katavi are you likely to see the rare and endangered Puku antelope, the gracious and scimitar-horned black Sable antelope, and the related Roan antelope with its shorter horns, tawny-red coat and white muzzle.

Six aerial surveys have been conducted from 1977 to 1998 in the ecosystem that includes the Katavi National Park and the Rukwa Game Reserve, a hunting preserve to the east and south of the park.

Sunset over the river

Opposite page: Vast herd of buffalo on the Katavi Plains

From the surveys it appears that substantial decreases have occurred in the buffalo, eland, hartebeest, roan/sable and zebra populations. In contrast, the number of elephant and giraffe appears to have increased dramatically while the populations of impala, waterbuck and topi remained fairly stable. However, because of the high margin of error in counting some species, meaningful comparison is not useful.

Katavi Plains lies about a third of the way up Lake Tanganyika and some 25 km to the east of the lake. It is a remote park to the northwest of Lake Rukwa and the town of Mbeya, both of which are in Tanzania's Southern Highlands.

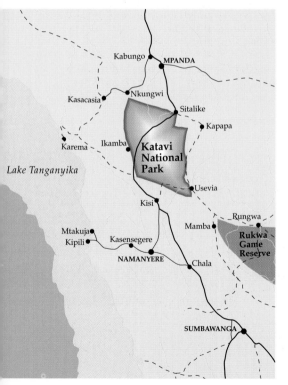

Getting to Katavi is difficult. For those from the south who have vehicles, the shortest route is through Mbala in Zambia, on to the regional capital of Sumbawanga in Tanzania, and then further north. Another route is to turn left soon after the border post at Tunduma. The current state of the dirt roads on both routes needs careful checking.

For visitors from the northern hemisphere, the best way to get to Katavi is to fly by charter plane, either from the Tanzania commercial capital of Dar es Salaam or the safari capital of Arusha. Alternatively, you can take lake transport to Karema in Tanzania.

Katavi Plains is cocooned from the rest of the country and the well-beaten tourist track by its very remoteness, and the access road system outside the park. As such, it becomes an expensive destination for tourists, although for many its greatest attraction is the scarcity of people.

About 450 species of birds have been seen in the area and 24 species of fish have been identified in Lake Rukwa. The fish include *Oreochromis rukwaensis*, an endemic of the lake that is also the most abundant. It is the species most able to survive the lake's fluctuations in level.

Crocodiles are very common in the lake although their numbers have been drastically reduced as a result of droughts and cropping. Large numbers of crocodiles exist in the Katuma and Kapapa rivers that flow into Lake Chada. Burrowing when the lake level drops, has become a survival response by the crocodiles.

Fluctuations in Lake Rukwa and other lakes in the area temporarily impacts on the wildlife. In 2002, there was a loss of 1,000 sq km of grazing land as a result of rising water at the northern end of Lake Rukwa. But once the lake recedes and the grasslands return, the species such as puku, topi and zebra will re-establish themselves.

Hippopotamus

Lake Rukwa's catchment area is over 85,000 sq km. For much of its recorded history it has been two separate lakes. Today it is one although the entire lake may have dried up entirely three times in the past 100 years.

Presently the lake is at a high level resulting in less grazing for the mammal population. This cycle appears to occur every 30 years with the resultant thinning in the wildlife. In contrast, Lakes Chada and Katavi appear to be receding with an increase in wild animals.

Roan antelope

Katavi National Park lies in a basin of the Great Rift Valley. Lyamba la Mpipa escarpment to the west and Mlele escarpment in the east border the park. A number of large hilly outcrops occur near the escarpment, a sign of their resistance to the process of weathering.

The basement geology of the region was laid two-and-a-half-billion years ago. The oldest rocks are part of the Dodoma system and are composed of silicate minerals (amphibolites), coarse-grained, banded crystalline rock (gneisses) and well-foliated, medium- to coarse-grained rock (schists).

The youngest deposits are to be found in the alluvial plains of the Rukwa Rift and they are a mere 3 million years old. Granite and dolerite are found throughout this area and are apparent in the eastern parts of Katavi National Park.

Potentially viable deposits of gold, iron, mica and silver exist in the area, as do small amounts of chrome, cobalt, lead and nickel. Gold is presently mined outside the park, as Tanzania has a policy of prohibiting mining inside park and reserve boundaries.

Soils derive from the parent rocks. They are generally sandy and the type of soil has important implications for the vegetation with the soils at the top of the ridges often rich in minerals while those further down contain iron and aluminum. Black clays tend to dominate in the valley bottoms.

All rivers in this area drain into Lake Rukwa. Because of the high inflows of salt, high evaporation and no outflow, the lake is saline.

While many rivers dry up after July, some residual pools may be fed by springs. The swamp and floodplain system is at the heart of Katavi Plains National Park.

A shallow table of water may cover much of these plains at the height of the rains. In the dry season, water resources are very limited, meaning that the wildlife concentrates and this has important implications for future tourist expansion.

Elephants at waterhole

Climate

The Katavi-Rukwa area should receive 900 to 1,000 mm of rainfall per annum. But early in 2002, the indications were that the area was having a drought with the average annual rainfall about one-third below normal.

In the years 1959 to 1979, the average rainfall for the area was 950 mm. But from 1980 to 1999, the average was 650 mm. In 1979, in excess of 2,000 mm of rain was received but in 1980 only 300 mm of rain was recorded.

October is the hottest month with average temperatures exceeding 30 degrees C in the Lake Rukwa area. June is the coolest month with the temperature dropping below 24 degrees C on the lakeshores.

A detailed inventory of the vegetation in the area has not been done. However, a detailed vegetation cover map of Tanzania does exist and this broadly classifies the area as *miombo* and mixed woodland.

Miombo is a loose term that covers much of southeast-central Africa from Zimbabwe in the south to northern Tanzania. The soils that support this type of vegetation are often shallow and stony with somewhat acidic contents. Mixed woodland is usually found below 1,000 metres or on alluvial soils.

Elevation affects the rainfall of an area and that further modifies the vegetation. Thus it can be argued that Katavi Plains has four principle types of vegetation.

In ascending order these are: grasslands and *mbugas,* mixed thickets, open woodland and *miombo* proper. *Miombo* can be further divided into plateau, escarpment and mixed, and there are riverine thickets and forests.

Lioness hunting

Plateau *miombo* is dense and in some places closed woodland. Here *Brachystegia* dominates whereas in escarpment *miombo* the dominant species of tree is *Julbernardia globiflora.* Mixed *miombo* contains fairly diverse species. In the mixed woodlands, *Combretum* and *Terminalia* are common.

Little has been written about the history and culture of the people in this area. Originally the area was the home of the Pimbwe, Rungwa and Bende peoples. But in the past 30 years other ethnic groups such as the Sukuma, Nyamwezi, and Fipa as well as Hutu and Tutsi refugees have entered the area.

These refugees today make up about 50 percent of the population of Mpanda District in which Katavi National Park accounts for almost 20 percent of the land area.

View across the Katavi Plains with waterbuck in the foreground

While the original groups relied heavily on wildlife resources and did not raise domestic livestock, the immigrants are largely agriculturalists (the refugees) and agro-pastoralists (the Sukuma). This latter group has introduced domestic livestock to the area thereby incurring the wrath of environmentalists.

The indigenous people of this area have a strong reputation for witchcraft. This is reflected in the name of the regional capital, Sumbawanga, that means in the Fipa language "throw away your witchcraft". This implies for the immigrants that if they bring their witchcraft with them they will not be able to compete with their hosts.

Mahale is on the eastern shore of Lake Tanganyika and is the least accessible of Tanzania's 14 national parks. This may be a blessing for its very remoteness helps to protect the population of over 700 chimpanzees as well as the park's rugged grandeur.

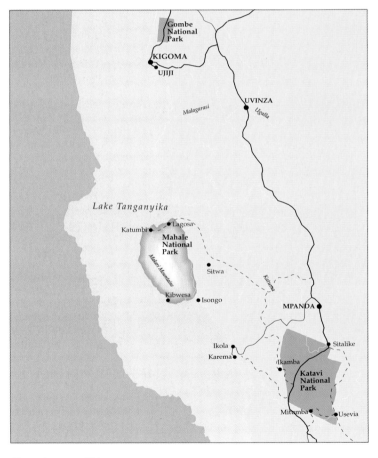

Opposite page: Chimpanzee

"Virgin nature can be found only in remote, truly uninhabited places, which are inaccessible by land routes. Mahale, which can only be reached by boat on Lake Tanganyika, happens to be one of those spots," wrote Dr Junichiro Itani, head of the Japanese team that prepared a study proposing Mahale be made a national park.

Mahale National Park

Mahale become a national park in 1985
It was the eleventh park Tanzania created
The size of the park is 1,613 sq km
This is a walking and camping park
It is on the eastern shore of Lake Tanganyika
The lake is the second deepest in the world
At 720 km, the lake is the world's longest
Lake Tanganyika is 54,400 sq km in size
Some 200 different fishes live in the lake
Nearly 90 percent of the fish are endemic.

The chimpanzee species at Mahale are Long-haired *(Pan troglodytes Schweinfurthii)*. They exist in fewer numbers at Gombe National Park to the north.

Only about 2,000 Long-haired chimpanzees survive in the wild. They are found in their greatest numbers on the western bank of the Malagarasi River, the largest flowing into eastern Lake Tanganyika. The chimpanzees range through several distinct areas covering 10,000 sq km. A large number of these areas are outside the park.

The population density of the chimpanzees depends upon the density of the tropical forest. Outside Mahale they are to be found in the western Lilanshimba area, the dry Ugalla area in the north where the Malagarasi River enters the park, and to a lesser extent in the Masito, Mukuyu, Karobwa and Wansisi areas.

Chimpanzees in a tree

The Japanese study of primates at Mahale has been continuous since 1961 when the first expedition from Kyoto University went to the area. Their mission throughout has been to ascertain the links between chimpanzees and humans.

The use of crude tools, once associated only with humans, has been seen frequently among Mahale chimpanzees. Different tools are used for various insects. A carefully selected narrow branch of a tree, vine or a grass stalk is inserted in a nest of ants like a fishing probe.

The ants stick to the probe and the chimpanzee licks them off. This exercise, mainly in October to December, may be repeated for an hour-and-a-half with up to 500 insertions of the probe occurring.

The use of such tools usually occurs during the afternoon when the chimpanzees are resting from the more intensive eating periods in the early morning and late afternoon, and the ants and other insects may provide a dietary supplement for the chimpanzees.

Chimpanzees awake between 0600 and 0800 daily. They stretch for 5 to 10 minutes before climbing down the tree and beginning an intensive feeding period on leaves and fruit. By roughly 1100 they have eaten enough and their rest commences, usually on the ground during the dry season or in a tree during the rains.

Grooming

Mutual grooming among the adults and playing by the younger chimpanzees then follows until the late afternoon when intensive feeding recommences. At night they sleep in the trees with adult chimpanzees being responsible for making their own bed.

Chimpanzees travel up to 5 km a day depending upon the availability of food and those at Mahale are at the southeastern edge of their range. Long-haired chimpanzees are also called Bald-headed chimpanzees.

Male chimpanzees weigh just over 50 kg each, females about 40 kg. Male torsos, including the head, vary from 80 to 90 cm; females from 70 to 80 cm. While the overall size is much smaller than that of humans, the prominent muscles of chimpanzees show their conspicuous body strength.

Lone chimpanzee

Tanzania National Parks (TANAPA) advises visitors never to feed chimpanzees (or any other wild animals), and to keep at least 5 metres from primates at all times because of human diseases being transmitted; warns the visitor who may be charged by a chimpanzee to hold on tightly to the nearest strong tree; and to respect chimpanzees at all times, never coming between a mother and her offspring.

Chimpanzees move in trees and on the ground. Knuckle-walking on all fours is their main means of moving from one place to another. But their eating is almost always confined to the trees where their preferred diet is leaves and fruit.

While their diet is basically vegetarian, they do have some carnivorous tendencies. These range through birds, eggs and small- to medium-sized mammals.

Only two possible predators of chimpanzees are thought to exist at Mahale: Leopards and Crowned hawk eagles. Eight other species of primates are found at Mahale (the most in any of Tanzania's national parks) and they normally give chimpanzees a wide berth.

The Angolan black-and-white colobus monkey is confined largely to the mountainous main ridge. But the others are frequently seen in the Kasoge area on the lakeshore. They include Red colobus that have a white tail, chubby Blue or Sykes monkeys, the Red-tailed and Vervet monkeys, as well as delicate Yellow baboons.

Two species of galagos or bushbabies also live in the area. They are the Greater Galago that, as its name suggests, is one of the largest bushbabies, and the Senegal Galago. The former has a thick tail while the latter has flat, large ears and large round eyes like a squirrel. Both are nocturnal.

Many of the hoofed animals may be seen in the eastern part of Mahale where *miombo* forest is dominant. These include Maasai giraffe, Grant's zebra, Lichtenstein's hartebeest (also known as Kongoni in Tanzania), and Spotted hyena. Among the smaller mammals are Cape hares and Chequered elephant shrews.

African elephants may be found around the Kabesi River to the east of Mahale's main ridge while many buffalo live in the

Blue or Sykes monkey

catchment area of the river and on a plateau in the southwest part of Mahale's main ridge. Large numbers of lions and African hunting dogs also live in this area.

Hippopotamus can be found near Myako, Sinsiba and Nganja while African clawless otters may be seen in the lake and Spot-necked otters in mountains streams that are rich in river crabs. Among the other nocturnal animals, African civets are seen at Myako camp.

In the montane forest, leopards are fairly common although rarely seen. Blue duikers, although essentially West African, are thought to exist at this point where east, west and southern African fauna and flora meet and overlap.

View of Mahale

The west of Tanzania consists of dry woodland savannah. This is locally known as *miombo*. It is characterized by sparsely distributed tall trees that form an outer perimeter around the tropical rain forests, and a dense covering of low trees and bush. About a quarter of the African continent, excluding deserts and lakes, is covered by *miombo*.

In Mahale, about three-quarters of the area is covered by *miombo* and the remainder by typical residual natural vegetation.

Birds inhabit Mahale according to their feeding patterns. For instance, waterbirds exist on or near the lake. These include: Little egrets, Goliath herons (which are the largest member of the heron family), Red-billed ducks, and black-and-white Pied kingfishers that hover before diving for their selected prey.

Pied kingfisher

Abandoned farmlands near the lake have been transformed into areas of secondary vegetation and grassland. Here numerous seedeaters are present such as weavers, sparrows and widow birds. You may also hear the Robin chats, White-browed coucals, Emerald-spotted wood doves and Tropical boubous.

In the neighbouring trees, you might catch a glimpse of the Green wood hoopoe, and you might observe the gruesome attacks on Mahale's many monkeys by the Crowned hawk eagle.

Kasoge forest and environs contains a multiplicity of birds ranging from the Dark-headed bulbul to Ross's turaco. Cuckoos exist in the forest, as do Rough-winged swallows. Crowned and trumpeter hornbill may also be seen.

On the mountain ridge, Olive pigeons, Red-winged and Violet-backed starlings, Black-headed orioles, Tawny eagles and White-naped ravens have been observed. In the *miombo* on the eastern slopes of the ridge, one may encounter Pennant-winged nightjar with their extremely long white tails, Drongos and the colourful Woodland kingfishers.

Mount Nkungwe that peaks at 2,462 metres is the highest point of the park where six peaks top 2,000 metres. The hilly country below contains several rapidly flowing streams that discharge their water into Lake Tanganyika.

Although the geological formation of the entire park occurred in the pre-Cambrian era (over 600 million years ago), strata of the Middle Stone Age are evident in two places at Mahale. The soil throughout the park is well-drained, sandy loam.

The dry season at Mahale lasts from approximately the end of May to the beginning of October with a rainy season covering the remainder of the year. Rainfall varies according to the distance from the lake although on average Mahale receives 800 mm to 1,000 mm of rain a year. The minimum recorded temperature occurs in August and the maximum in October.

The human residents of Mahale Mountains and environs are Tongwe, Bende and Waholoholo. They are shifting cultivators belonging to the "Nyamwezi cluster". The Nyamwezi trace their origins to the Congo having crossed Lake Tanganyika in small, dugout canoes.

The Nyamwezi were the porters who carried ivory and other export goods from the interior. Nyamwezi is Swahili meaning "the people of the moon". It is thought the name was given to them by the coastal people because they came from the west.

Boat and Lake Tanganyika

RUBONDO ISLAND NATIONAL PARK

Rubondo Island is only a dot of land in 69,490 sq km Lake Victoria, Africa's largest lake and second in the world behind Lake Superior on the Canada-US border. But, as anyone who has been to Rubondo can tell you, the island is a hidden paradise.

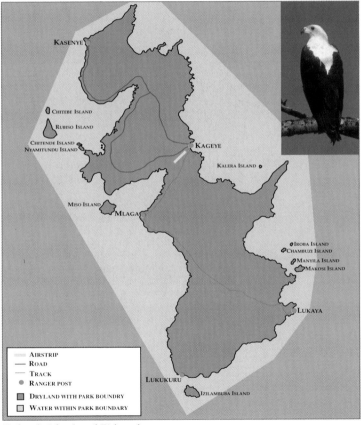

Rubondo Island; and Fish eagle

Opposite page: Elephant drinking on a Rubondo beach

Lake Victoria, its eastern shore only a few km from the Serengeti, is the unheralded giant of Tanzanian tourism. It is a historically rich region with Late Stone Age rock shelters and prehistoric art. Today the people are dependent upon fishing, minerals, cotton and coffee for their livelihood. The Sukuma around Mwanza are Tanzania's largest ethic group.

Brief profile

Created in 1977 from a game reserve
The park covers an area of 456.8 sq km
Of the total area, 236.8 sq km are land
There are 11 smaller offshore islands
It is 26 km in length and 10 km in width
Rubondo is Tanzania's only island park.

Tanzania lies on a plateau rising to 1,333 metres above sea level with Lake Victoria at just over 1,100 metres. Billions of years ago, this area was part of a vast flat plain sloping gently towards the sea.

A tectonic upheaval dislocated the plain elevating part of the surrounding terrain and creating the world's largest known diamond-bearing kimberlite pipe and many other gemstones. Rock outcrops *(kopjes)* stud the area.

The fastest means of getting to Rubondo Island is by charter plane. The waves in the lake below reveal the muddy-brown colour of the shallow water that is interspersed by many islands, some liberally sprinkled with whitened bird droppings.

After a 30-minute flight from Mwanza to Rubondo, my pilot skimmed the lake in search of crocodiles. Only feet away, it seemed, two enormous crocodiles lay basking in the sun on a mud bank.

Then the pilot buzzed the island's grass airstrip at low altitude. "No animals on it today," he announced over the earphones. The island's only two permitted vehicles were waiting beside the bush runway; a 4x4 belonging to TANAPA and a similar one for the island's only tented camp.

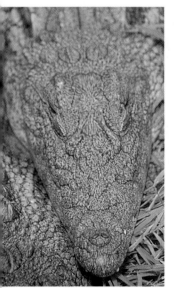

The different colours of a Nile crocodile

From the air was a glimpse of the green mantle of trees that cloaks most of Rubondo. Inconspicuous from the air were the animals and birds that the foliage conceals. Some of these are to be seen on the brief drive to Rubondo Island Camp.

Bushbucks, robust but elegant Sitatunga (once called Marshbuck) that are unique to the island, vervet and black-and-white colobus monkeys all greet the visitors. The high-pitched screeches and whistles of Grey parrots reverberate through the forest.

From 1965 to 1973, Professor Bernard Grzimek of the Frankfurt Zoological Society treated Rubondo as his own private sanctuary. He introduced wildlife considered to be rare or endangered. The island provided "a wilderness refuge for species threatened with extinction", was how Frankfurt put it.

Sixteen black rhinoceros (later poached in the 1970s), giraffe, black-and-white colobus monkeys, roan antelope (now extinct because the habitat is unsuitable), suni that are the smallest antelopes in Africa, and six elephants, were introduced.

It defies logic, then and now, why anyone would want to introduce elephants (or for that matter other non-endangered species), when Tanzania in those days had well over 100,000 elephants. Today Rubondo's 40 elephants threaten the fragile forest habitat.

African grey parrot

Frankfurt's designs were finally terminated after the introduction of 17 unwanted chimpanzees from European zoos and circuses. They were classified as "problem" animals in Europe and their rarely seen offspring still exist on Rubondo.

Of greater relevance, suggested the Tanzania Game Division in a 1977 report, would be the introduction of endangered east African forest species such as golden cats that are twice the size of the domestic species, hyrax, giant forest hogs, yellow-backed duikers, Abbot's duikers, red colobus and mangabey monkeys, flying squirrels and tree pangolins.

Rubondo had (and has) plenty of indigenous wildlife. The Sitatunga is the most notable of these. Its scientific name is *Tragelaphus spekei*, named after explorer, John Hanning Speke, who discovered the source of the White Nile River.

Sitatunga

Sitatunga are somewhat larger than the bushbuck. They have longer and more twisted horns, white vertical stripes and darker, shaggier and longer coats that are oily and water-repellant. They are higher in the back than the front giving a somewhat hunched impression.

They are truly aquatic animals usually found in the papyrus and reed swamps that surround Rubondo although in the confined and predator-free space they frequently occur inland in the forests.

Their long, splayed hooves and flexible ankle joints are adapted to support them on soft, boggy and marsh vegetation without sinking into the ground. They are good but slow swimmers, and when surprised they may submerge with only the end of their snouts protruding so they can breath.

At Rubondo Island the visitor is almost certain to see the nocturnal Large-spotted or Blotched genet. They will appear at night from the rocks just behind the bar that joins the open-air dining room at the camp.

They have short legs, sharp, curved and retractable claws and the underlying coat varies from brownish grey to pale yellowish or buff-white with the large and elongated spots being darker in colour.

They are active mainly in the evenings or on moonlit nights and they tend to be solitary, with rodents as their main staple food. Their diet can extend to birds, bats, lizards, snakes and fish as well as other smaller morsels such as grasshoppers, moths, spiders, centipedes and scorpions.

Genet

Another animals you may see at Rubondo Island are the Spot-necked otters. It is the smallest but best swimmer of this species with its feet entirely webbed and adapted for swimming. On land it is the least mobile of the otters.

They are very curious animals given to popping up their heads to observe people who are observing them. They are highly aquatic animals, devouring slow-moving fish, and they vigorously defend their stretch of shore, producing three offspring.

As one would expect on an island, most of the birds are aquatic. A boat trip to "Bird Island" is a must, best combined with a meander around Rubondo itself. Tens of thousands of birds, among them cormorants and egrets, migrate to the island daily from their feeding grounds elsewhere.

The island is a bewildering confetti-like blur as the birds roost every day high above the numerous crocodiles. The sky is almost blackened as the birds disputatiously seek their roosts.

On the way to "Bird Island", Goliath herons may be seen skulking while Fish eagles emit their haunting and mournful call from the treetops. Sacred ibis are common on the foreshore together with Open-billed stork and migrant species on their annual pilgrimage overlap with a variety of indigenous birds.

Birds roost at sunset on Lake Victoria

Lake Victoria

Lake Victoria, a shallow-flooded depression, lies between the eastern and western arms of the Great Rift Valley that crosses Africa. The lake is 337 km in length and 240 km wide. Africans call it Nyanza while the early Arab slavers called it Ukerewe after one of its many islands.

The lake contained what a Briton described as "the greatest geographical secret after the discovery of America". That secret was the source of the White Nile River that emerges into the Mediterranean Sea through Sudan and Egypt.

The White Nile begins it long journey to the Mediterranean from Lake Victoria

To Victorian Europe, obsessed with exploration, the source of the mighty river excited both passion and controversy. On 3 August 1858, Speke, peering across the vast expanse of water near Mwanza, pronounced that he had found the source of the White Nile.

His inspired guess, for that is all it could have been, provoked a disbelieving reaction in London. His fellow explorer, John Burton, who had also sought the source of the Nile, denounced Speke's "discovery" as being unscientific.

David Livingstone who got most things wrong in Africa , took Burton's side. "Poor Speke has turned his back on the real source of the Nile," he wrote. "His river at Ripon Falls was not large enough for the source of the Nile."

Speke had named Ripon Falls after the head of the Royal Geographical Society who funded his journey. But it was 17 years (and only after Speke's death) before his blunt statement that he had found the source of the Nile was vindicated.

English-born American journalist, Henry Morton Stanley, who sailed around Lake Victoria, later wrote: "I must give him [Speke] credit for having understood the geography of the countries we travelled through better than any of those who so persistently opposed his hypothesis." He had written Speke's valedictory posthumously and silenced the powerful disbelievers.

The lake contains an estimated 1 million tonnes of fish. Of this total, 650,000 tonnes are Nile perch, 150,000 tonnes *dagaa* (a Swahili word for small fish like whitebait) that is sun-dried, 100,000 tonnes of tilapia and 100,000 tonnes for the remaining 200 species.

The sweet-tasting tilapia is the most popular fish around the lake. Nile perch is the main export fish from the region and giant cargo planes wait at Mwanza airport to airlift the fillets of Nile perch to the European Union, Asia and the Middle East.

Two-thirds of the lakes fishers target Nile perch. At night their lights bob up and down on the lake that can frequently be very turbulent with thunderstorm velocities exceeding 70 knots. Factories surround the lake where the fish are cleaned before being filleted and boxed for shipping.

One of the most valuable parts of the Nile perch is its swim bladder, the organ enabling it to rise and sink in the water. The swim bladders are sent to England for filtering beer and wine, and they are used in the Far East for thickening soup. The Nile perch's sandpapery hide is also used to make sandals, purses and wallets.

Lake Victoria, in common with much of Tanzania, has two rainy seasons. Because the lake is so large, rainfall patterns vary enormously. Rubondo Island averages 1,200 mm per annum. However, even when it is raining, the weather is pleasant with temperatures reaching a high of 26 degrees C and a low of 16 degrees C.

Fishers on Lake Victoria at sunset

FACILITIES/WHERE TO STAY

Before you pack, you need to decide how you are getting to Tanzania, how to get around the country and where to stay. Many airlines internationally and regionally service Tanzania, and there are innumerable safari operators to get you around the country and places to stay that your travel agent should be able to advise you about.

But don't take as gospel the advice your travel agent gives. Many are not Africa specialists. And even those whom you may think know everything will have certain preferred carriers or places to stay as a result of getting a "freebie" or a special discount. So shopping around should be your first option.

There is at least one flight a day to Tanzania from Europe and several from the Middle East and Africa. While internally there is a national carrier, Precision Air based in Arusha is the most reliable domestic commercial carrier and has the most convenient schedules. Coastal Air from Dar es Salaam has the best internal charter coverage with the added advantage that some of their flights operate commercially.

The following gives you a guide to some of the facilities in Tanzania. The list below is not definitive. But they are recommended. The facilities listed appear in alphabetical order under commercial airlines and charter companies, where to stay in northern, coastal, southern and western Tanzania. There follows a listing of some of the main internal safari operators and the Tanzanian agents for African Publishing Group International.

Several of these hotels, lodges and tented camps have facilities beyond the section where they are listed. Foxes African Safaris, for example, has the Lazy Lagoon off Bagamoyo as its coastal facility, Mikumi, Mufindi and Ruaha on the southern circuit plus a train service, and Katavi on the western circuit. But their headquarters are on the southern circuit.

All places listed here have same-day laundry services and the in-town places usually have telephones in the rooms, televisions and various other amenities. Most bush lodges and tented camps consider that visitors have come to see the fauna and flora and not to be interrupted by the telephone or the television.

Opposite page: Paradise flycatcher

A word of warning about the safari operator you choose. Make sure they are members of the Tanzanian Association of Tour Operators (TATO) as some of those who are not tend to have poor equipment and dubious reputations. By choosing your operator from the TATO list you will be sparing yourself possible frustration and helping the authorities stamp out malpractices.

Not all visitors to Tanzania may wish to stay in the hotels, lodges or tented camps or travel with a registered safari operator. Alternatives do exist although finding them can be time-consuming.

You can travel in an overland truck, hire your own car, you can go by bus, train or boat, you can hire a bicycle and you can even hitchhike. You can stay at cheaper accommodation or camp in many of the parks or reserves. But this requires considerable planning and is usually not considered by American and European travellers who have two to three week holiday periods.

All Tanzanian telephone numbers begin with 255, that is the country code. From overseas for mobile/cell phones, you simply dial 255 followed by the number of the company (744, 748, 741 etc), and then the number you are calling.

For calling fixed telephones or "landlines" from outside Tanzania, you dial 255 followed by the Dar es Salaam number 22 and then the number you are calling. Arusha, Moshi, Usa River and Kilimanjaro International Airport (KIA) have 27 after the 255 and before the number you are calling, Bukoba and Kigoma have 28 and Iringa 26.

With mobile/cell calls from inside Tanzania, you add a 0 before the town you want while dropping the country code. Thus, Arusha becomes 027 followed by the number you are calling.

DOMESTIC AIRLINES & CHARTER COMPANIES

Coastal Aviation, Box 3052, Dar es Salaam. Tel: 2843293 or 2842877. E-mail: aviation@coastal.cc Web: www.coastal.cc Flies commercially three times a day into the Selous: once from Dar es Salaam, once from Mafia Island and once from Zanzibar. It also connects the Selous to Ruaha National Park and Arusha three times a week.

Precision Air, Box 1636, Arusha. Tel: 2506903. Fax: 2508204. E-mail: pwmarketing@precisionairtz.com Web: www.precisionairtz.com Flies return daily to: Dar es Salaam-Zanzibar-Arusha; Bukoba-Mwanza-Bukoba; Dar es Salaam-Zanzibar-Mombasa. Other destinations include: Entebbe, Grumeti, Lake Manyara, Seronera, Nairobi, Kilimanjaro, Mtwara, Tabora, Kigoma, Shinyanga, Pemba, Mafia and Lindi.

HOTELS, LODGES & TENTED CAMPS

Arusha & Northern Tanzania

Dik Dik Hotel-Tours, Box 1499, Arusha. Tel: 2553499. Fax: 2553498. E-mail: dikdik@atge.automail.com Web: www.dikdik.com Located at Usa River midway between Arusha airport and Kilimanjaro International Airport (KIA), this hotel has excellent cuisine and is a most relaxing starting point for climbing Africa's highest peak, snow-capped Mount Kilimanjaro, and for all your safaris.

Impala Hotel, Box 7302, Arusha. Tel: 2508448/51. Fax: 2508220. E-mail: impala@cybernet.co.tz Web: www.impalahotel.com Located a km from Arusha centre, the Impala has 160 ensuite rooms with colour TVs, direct dial telephones, daily laundry, a bureau de change, travel operator, internet café, secretarial services and conference facilities. Continental, Chinese, Italian and Indian food is served in four restaurants.

KIA Lodge, Kilimanjaro International Airport, Box 43, KIA, Arusha. Tel: 2554194/5. Fax: 2554196. E–mail: kialodge@africaonline.co.tz Web: www.kialodge.africaonline.co.tz On a secluded hill only 3 minutes from the airport, this hotel has spectacular views of Mount Kilimanjaro. It contains 40 air-conditioned rooms, a restaurant, bar, lounge, pool, internet, conference facilities and a business centre.

Moivaro Coffee Plantation Lodge and Restaurant, Box 11297, Arusha. Tel: 2553326. Fax: 2553242. E-mail: reservations@moivaro.com Web: www.moivaro.com In a natural setting 7 km from Arusha, this coffee plantation has spectacular views of Mount Meru. The lodge has 25 picturesque cottages for guests, a restaurant, bar, lounge, swimming pool, massage room and internet facilities.

Mount Meru Hotel, Box 877, Arusha. Tel: 2502711/2. Fax: 2508503. E-mail: sales-novotel@cybernet.co.tz Web: www.tahi.co.tz Close to the town centre, this 3-star 168 room hotel, has Mount Meru as its backdrop and overlooks the golf course. Close to Arusha airport and 45 km from Kilimanjaro International Airport (KIA), it has two restaurants, a spacious lobby, pool snack bar and conference facilities for 150 delegates.

Ndutu Safari Lodge, Box 6084, Arusha. Tel: 2508930. Fax: 2508310. Email: ndutu@bushlink.co.tz Web: www.ndutu.com Just inside Ngorongoro in the southern Serengeti ecosystem, this lodge nestles under *Acacia* trees and overlooks a soda lake. Each year the 34 stone cottages, open-sided bar, lounge and dining room, are surrounded by some 2 million animals making Ndutu one of the best places to watch wildlife.

Ngare Sero Mountain Lodge, Box 425, Arusha. Tel: 2553638. E-mail: reservations@Ngare-Sero-Lodge.com Web: Ngare-Sero-Lodge.com Stylish country house, base for safaris, set amidst forest and lake with profusion of birds, troops of monkeys, trout fishing and horse riding. Experience the sun setting on the glaciers of Kilimanjaro. Close to Arusha National Park and between Kilimanjaro and Arusha airports.

Oliver's Camps, Box 425, Arusha. Tel: (744) 465473. E-mail: olivers@habari.co.tz Web: www.oliverscamp.com Twenty years of experience of guiding make this an unforgettable experience. You feel at home from your arrival as only a valued guest of Paul Oliver and his guides can be. The camps are small and intimate and your own guide takes you on an adventure in a private vehicle during your visit to Tarangire or Sanjan.

Protea Hotel Aishi Machame, Box 534, Moshi. Tel: 2756948. Fax: 2756821. E-mail: proteaaishi@africaonline.co.tz Web: www.proteahotels.com/aishi Seven km from the scenic Machame ascent, this elegant 30-bedroom hotel with a heated swimming pool and fitness centre at last offers luxury accommodation for climbers of Mount Kilimanjaro, beautiful gardens and easy access to guests exploring Tanzania's northern safari circuit.

Rivertrees Country Inn, Box 235, Arusha. Tel: 2553894. Fax: 2553893. E-mail: rivertrees@africaonline.co.tz   Web: www.rivertrees.com Charming old farmhouse in the country with 8 ensuite guest rooms and 2 river cottages with log-fires in natural gardens near the Usa River. Abounds with birdlife and has spectacular views of Mounts Kilimanjaro and Meru. Swimming pool, restaurant, country food, pub and hospitality.

Sopa Lodges, Box 1823, Arusha. Tel: 2500630/9. Fax: 2508245. E-mail: info@sopalodges.com   Web: www.sopalodges.com Unsurpassed hospitality in the heart of East Africa. Sopa has lodges in Tarangire, host to northern Tanzania's largest elephant herd; Ngorongoro, home of the Big Five; and Serengeti, with its great wildebeest migration. Sopa Lodges – the base upon which a never forgotten experience is built.

Tanzania Hotel Investments (TAHI), Box 877, Arusha. Tel: 2502711/2. Fax: 2508505. E-mail: sales-novotel@cybernet.co.tz Web: www.tahi.co.tz Seronera Wildlife Lodge and Lobo Wildlife Lodge in the Serengeti, Ngorongoro Wildlife Lodge, and Lake Manyara Hotel guarantee you northern Tanzania's spectacular wildlife, birds and flora, while the Mafia Island Lodge is strategically located for discerning sea lovers.

Tarangire Safari Lodge, Box 2703, Arusha. Tel: 2544222. E-mail: sss@habari.co.tz Web: www.tarangiresafarilodge.com Set above the park, visitors can watch elephants and other animals in the Tarangire River below, see Bateleur eagles wheeling overhead and photograph resident monkeys and squirrels. The atmosphere is friendly, the twin-bedded ensuite tents are comfortable, and there is a pool and shop.

The Arusha Hotel, Box 88, Arusha. Tel: 250777 or 2508870/3. Fax: 2508889. Mobile: 747265. E-mail: marketing@newarusha.com Just re-opened and completely renovated and refurbished, this hotel is the perfect way to begin and end a safari. The landscaped gardens with a heated swimming pool and all amenities, are designed for the discerning traveller. Professional, attentive service matches international standards.

Dar es Salaam & Southern Tanzania

Foxes African Safaris, Box 10270, Dar es Salaam. Tel/fax: (744) 237422. E-mail: fox@tanzaniasafaris.info Web: www.tanzaniasafaris.info No group in Tanzania has such a diversity of products. Foxes African Safaris encompass owner-managed camps in Katavi, Mikumi and Ruaha parks, freshwater fishing in the Mufindi tea estates and swimming on a pristine Indian Ocean island, plus their own train to Mikumi and Selous.

Holiday Inn, Box 80022, Dar es Salaam. Tel: 2137575. Fax: 2139070. E-mail: hidar@hidar.co.tz Web: www.holiday-inn.com/daressalaam In Garden Avenue close to the city centre, and near the national museum, botanical gardens and seafront, this quiet hotel has 152 ensuite rooms with all amenities, two fully serviced restaurants, the latest equipment for seminars and conferences, a curio shop, travel and business centre.

Mwagusi Safari Camp, Box 369, Iringa. E-mail: ruahapark@bushlink.co.tz Web: www.ruaha.org Located in a transition zone where east and southern African fauna and flora overlap, this is Africa at its finest. Chris Fox was born and bred in the region and Mwagusi's 16 ensuite thatched bandas in Ruaha and the camp's ambience reveal his deep affinity with this vast, unspoilt wilderness that protects a wide variety of species.

Royal Palm, Box 971, Dar es Salaam. Tel: 2112416. Fax: 2113981. E-mail: royalpalm@cats-net.com Web: www.royalpalmdar.com Unquestionably the premier estabishment in Dar es Salaam offering true international standards and services. Centrally located in the heart of the business district of Dar es Salaam, it is within walking distance of most major office blocks and only 10 minutes drive from the airport.

Rufiji River Camp/Hippotours and Safaris, Box 13824, Dar es Salaam. Tel: 2128662/3. Fax: 2128661. E-mail: info@hippotours.com Web: www.hippotours.com The camp has 20 ensuite tents overlooking the Rufiji River in Selous. Excellent options for boat and foot activities including overnight fly camping, and game drives. Well stocked bar and Italian cuisine adds to the informal, relaxed atmosphere.

Saadani Safari Lodge, Box 105854, Dar es Salaam. Tel/fax: 2600867. E-mail: info@saadani.net   Web: www.saadani.net   This luxury, refurbished lodge is in the park nearest to Dar es Salaam. It has 9 ensuite beachfront cottages including a honeymoon suite. The restaurant serves international and local cuisine, including famous Saadani prawns, while the tree house is idyllic to read and watch game at the waterhole.

Sand Rivers Selous, Box 681, Usa River, Arusha. Tel/fax: (255.27) 2553819/20. E-mail: sara@nomad.co.tz Web: www.sandrivers.com Eight open-fronted thatched cottages overlook the Rufiji River blending the beauty of the Selous with comforts of the reserve's most upmarket lodge. Its very remoteness coupled with excellent food, fly camping, walking safaris and memorable river expeditions ensure an unforgettable visit.

Selous Impala, Box 3052, Dar es Salaam. Tel: 2117959/60. E-mail: safari@coastal.cc   Opened under new management in late 2003, this camp has 6 spacious tents on the banks of the majestic Rufiji River in Selous. Each tent has its own boat and safari 4x4 vehicle. From Selous Impala adventurous guests can descend the Rufiji River to the Indian Ocean, cross to Mafia Island, and from there catch a flight to Zanzibar or Dar es Salaam.

Western Tanzania

Chada Katavi, Box 681, Usa River, Arusha. Tel/fax: 2553819/20. E-mail: sara@nomad.co.tz Web: www.mahale.co.tz   In one of the wildest places on earth in the heart of a million acres of animals lies Chada Katavi camp. It is a stunningly located bush camp accommodating a maximum of 12 visitors. Its activities include walking safaris, game drives in open vehicles and overnight fly camping. Open June to March.

Gombe Tented Camp, Box 1160, Kigoma. Tel: 2804435/6/7. Fax: 2804434. E-mail: info@chimpanzeesafaris.com   Web: www.chimpanzeesafaris.com This semi-permanent tented camp at the northern end of Gombe on the lakeshore is the only one in the park. Operated by Chimpanzee Safaris, owners of the Kigoma Hilltop Hotel, who arrange guided walks/tracking to view chimpanzees as well as snorkeling and fishing.

Greystoke Mahale, Box 681, Usa River, Arusha. Tel/fax: 2553819/20. E–mail: sara@nomad.co.tz   Web: www.mahale.co.tz   In unspoilt tropical mountains, rivers and beaches on the shores of Lake Tanganyika, this is the finest place to watch chimpanzees. The stylish and comfortable camp accommodates 12 visitors. Activities include chimpanzee tracking, dhow trips, snorkeling, boat trips and fishing. Open June to March.

Nkungwe Tented Camp, Box 1160, Kigoma.   Tel: 2804435/6/7. Fax: 2804434.   E-mail: info@chimpanzeesafaris.com   Web: www.chimpanzeesafaris.com Semi-permanent tented camp on a long stretch of white sand beach at the centre of Mahale NP on Lake Tanganyika. Operated by Chimpanzee Safaris, owners of the Kigoma Hilltop Hotel, who arrange guided walks to view chimpanzees, snorkeling, fishing and mountaineering.

Tanganyika Swiss Hotels, Box 591, Arusha. Tel: 2548261. E-mail: flycat@habari.co.tz   Web: www.flycat.com   The nature lovers' hideaways: Rubondo Island Camp has 10 tents, a pool, boat/foot excursions and fishing; Katavi and Mahale camps are seasonal (July/October) with game drives, foot safaris, chimpanzee tracking and goggling.

SAFARI OPERATORS

Coastal Travels, Box 3052, Dar es Salaam.   Tel: 2117959/60.   Fax: 2118647.   E-mail: safari@coastal.cc Specializes in creating new destinations for the adventurous traveller. Latest project: Rubondo Island National Park in Lake Victoria. Robondo offers true unexplored wilderness, the very best in game viewing and world-class fishing.

Kiroyera Tours, Box 485, Bukoba.   Tel: 2220203.   E-mail: info@kiroyeratours.com Web: www.kiroyeratours.com The leading tourist company in Bukoba town on the western shore of Lake Victoria that promotes ecotourism in the area and to the nearby equator. Kiroyera Tours is located in the town centre where the desired itinerary of the visitor always comes first in experiencing the splendor of this land of plenty.

Kudu Safaris, Box 1404, Arusha. Tel: 2506065. Fax: 2508108. E-mail: kudu@habari.co.tz Kudu Safaris is a well-established company with personalized service, excellent guides and its own fleet of Landcruisers. They can arrange all your safari needs with private itineraries or set weekly departures, either by road or air, to lodges and luxury camps throughout Tanzania.

Leopard Tours, Box 1638, Arusha. Tel: 2508441/3. Fax: 2508219. E-mail: leopard@yako.habari.co.tz Web: www.leopard-tours.com Operates 140 safari vehicles, mostly stretched 4x4, with long-range call radios linked to Arusha HQ and offices in Dar es Salaam and Ngorongoro. Lodge and camping safaris, incentives, beach holidays, cultural visits and Kilimanjaro trekking, all with trademark personalized services.

Roy Safaris, Box 50, Arusha. Tel: 2502115. Fax: 2548892. E-mail: roysafaris@intafrica.com Web: www.roysafaris.com Established family business with 26 4WD vehicles driven by trained and experienced drivers/guides, with HF radios, reference books, binoculars and cool boxes. Specializes in lodge and camping safaris, walking safaris, mountain treks on Kilimanjaro and Meru, and beach holidays.

Safari Makers, Box 12902, Arusha. Tel: 2544446. E-mail: safarimakers@habari.co.tz Web: www.safarimakers.com Offering camping and lodge safaris to all Tanzanian national parks, Ngorongoro, the Selous and other game reserves, mountain climbing expeditions, cultural visits and beach holidays. Budget-to-luxury standard. Fully licensed tour operator and member of the Tanzania Association of Tour Operators.

Serengeti Balloon Safaris, Box 12116, Arusha. Tel: 2508578. Fax: 2548997. E-mail: info@baloonsafaris.com Web: www.balloonsafaris.com The ultimate safari experience. Launch at dawn and float gently over the heart of the Serengeti. Enjoy a unique perspective of the spectacular wildlife and scenary. Then touch down to a traditional champagne bush breakfast. Space is limited and advance bookings are recommended.

Sunny Safaris, Box 7267, Arusha. Tel: 2508184. Fax: 2548037. E-mail: info@sunnysafaris.com   Web: www.sunnysafaris.com Ranging from the snowcapped peaks of Kilimanjaro to the vast plains of the Serengeti, Sunny Safaris offers lodge safaris, budget camping safaris, mountain climbing, walking and mountain biking safaris and beach holidays to such exotic resorts as Zanzibar where it also has an office.

Tanzania Serengeti Adventure, Box 1742, Arusha. Tel: 2544609. Fax: 2508475. E-mail: tsa@habari.co.tz Web: www.habari.co.tz/tsa This official tour operator specializes in customized and scheduled safari programmes (mobile/permanent camps and lodges) to national parks, Kilimanjaro climbs, Zanzibar beaches and chimpanzee visits. Their guides specialize in birds, animals, plants, culture and climbing.

AFRICAN PUBLISHING GROUP
AGENT FOR NORTHERN TANZANIA

Jambo Coffee House and Makuti Gardens, Box 11478, Arusha. Mobile: (744) 305430. E-mail: smales@yahoo.com This coffee house and restaurant, the first in Arusha, was opened by Linda Smales who is APG's northern Tanzania agent. The establishment on Boma Road in Arusha is a fitting and inexpensive beginning and ending to a Tanzanian safari as well as a convenient meeting place.

AFRICAN PUBLISHING GROUP
AGENT FOR SOUTHERN TANZANIA

Saadani Safari Lodge, Box 105854, Dar es Salaam. Tel/fax: 2600867. E-mail: info@saadani.net   Web: www.saadani.net This luxury, refurbished lodge is in the park nearest to Dar es Salaam. It has 9 ensuite beachfront cottages including a honeymoon suite. The restaurant serves international and local cuisine, including famous Saadani prawns, while the tree house is idyllic to read and watch game at the waterhole.

WHAT TO TAKE AND DO

Having decided that you are going to Tanzania for your African safari, the next question for most people is what should they take?

First of all, carefully choose what you are carrying your safari items in, not just for the trip to Africa, but also for yourself and for those who may have to carry it in Tanzania. A canvas bag with good locks will suffice. Solid suitcases are burdensome for all concerned.

Your choice of clothing is mainly dictated by the climate that you encounter.

In the winter months of June and July, a light sweater or windcheater is strongly advised. For the warmer remainder of the year, lightweight clothing in environmentally-friendly colouring such as light khaki or green is recommended.

However, if you are climbing Mount Kilimanjaro or Meru, warm clothing is necessary all year round. This should include a balaclava and gloves for the very cold night conditions, as well as sun-protective items such as barrier cream and dark glasses for the daytime sun.

For those who are camping at one of the approved grounds, the choice is more optional. Tents and sleeping bags are necessary if you are not sleeping in the vehicle, and you will need your food and drink. Extra fuel is also a good idea and a fire at night should keep animals at bay.

Almost all safari facilities have same-day laundry so you can travel with no more than three changes of clothes in the bush: one in the laundry, one that you are wearing and a spare set in the cupboard.

Short-sleeved shirts or T-shirts are the norm and shorts or long trousers are acceptable. But you may want a long sleeved shirt and long trousers at night to keep the mosquitoes at bay. Sandals or tackies by day are also acceptable although once again, boots or shoes with ankle socks are advised at night.

Hats are very much a matter of choice. But you will need one that protects you from the rays of the hot lunchtime sun. And you will also need sunglasses.

So that has basically kitted you out. Now you have to decide what additional items you need to bring.

You may want to pack cameras, lenses or video camera of your choice. An adequate supply of film, batteries and cleaning equipment (the dust is pervasive) is advised. Many places you will stay have shops with films and batteries as well as other tourist mementos.

But these shops tend to be expensive and may not contain your first choice so packing what initially may seem like too much film, will not do any harm. You would also be advised to get your film processed on your return.

Binoculars, preferably lightweight, are very important. A lightweight but powerful torch is another essential, particularly as most safari camps turn off their generators at a given time each night.

Check with your hosts where you are staying whether the drinking water is safe; it should be at most safari destinations. Beyond that you can purchase bottles of drinking water or soft drinks at all reputable establishments.

The salads and other vegetables and fruit should also be quite safe to eat at safari facilities. But if you are personally buying them at a market or from a roadside vendor, make sure they are well washed before consuming. Remember at all times that those who have lived in the tropics for years have hardier stomachs than visitors.

Another thing to bring with you is your medical kit. Consult your local doctor well in advance of departure for advice on what prophylactics you should take for malaria prevention. Insect repellants and sun-cream will also be necessary.

Beyond that, your medical kit should include painkillers, pills for an upset stomach, band-aids and whatever your local practitioner advises.

In cases of emergency, the Flying Doctor Service is on call by most safari establishments and it is as well to have insurance to cover this expensive but unlikely eventuality.

Tour guides will escort most visitors around the park. But if you are hiring a self-drive car it is as well to take a guide from the park offices to maximize viewing and to ensure that you do not get lost.

If you must talk at all when viewing an animal, do so very quietly as the sound you make carries for a long distance and will frighten the animal and irritate other people. Approaching an animal slowly, and preferably obliquely, will frighten it less.

Remember always that patience is a virtue. By simply rushing up to an animal, taking a quick picture and then heading towards the next animal, you may miss the memorable picture you want.

Tanzania is a very informal country that respects one's religious faith. Therefore your eating and drinking habits are not curtailed. But it is appropriate to respect Tanzanian feelings when it comes to dress, particularly when you come from the beach.

The short or light rains occur from about November with the heavier rains in March until May. All the parks have good all-weather dirt roads but access to some of the more remote areas could be affected during the heavy rains.

Visitors at all time must follow park regulations. Beyond paying for entry, visitors should never: throw away lit cigarettes in case they start a fire, throw away litter, feed wild animals, disturb animals, birds or other visitors, pick flowers or destroy vegetation, bring pets or firearms into the park, or persuade the driver to leave the demarcated roads for a better view or picture.

Such demarcation is laid down to protect the often fragile environment. By crossing it in a vehicle to get a closer view of some animal, you threaten to irrepairably destroy the environment for future generations.

Also ensure that your driver/guide abides by the speed limits. These are laid down for very specific purposes and you are much more likely to see wildlife and appreciate your surroundings by travelling slowly than you are at speed.

Above all, you must never alight from the vehicle except at designated points. Wild animals can be very dangerous in protection of their young and their environment.

Game viewing is dictated by luck for it is impossible to guarantee that a given species will be in an area at a certain time. But you can make much of the luck yourself by properly preparing for your safari and listening when you reach your African destination.

Most safari facilities have early morning and late evening game drives. This is when the wildlife emerges from the shade of the trees where they have rested overnight or from the midday sun, and then grazes or prepares for its nocturnal activities.

So going on these drives is important for you will have probably paid a great deal of money for what you are about to see and you will see little by remaining in your camp.

You should try to look through the bush and not at individual trees and this is where binoculars are vital. You are looking for silhouettes and shadows, for anything that seems somewhat out of place or moves, perhaps a lion's ear or a leopard's tail. Maybe the unusual will be a termite mound, a bush or a log. Sometimes it will be an animal.

Your driver/guide will be more experienced in game spotting than you are. But you should try to supplement his or her efforts and never be afraid to ask questions. Remember there is no such thing as a silly question in the bush; only a silly answer.

You can judge the calibre of your driver/guide on the basis of their answers and this will help you determine the size of their tip at the end of your journey.

Your driver/guide may not know the answers immediately to all your questions. But a good driver/guide will consult once they get back to the facility where you are staying and give you the answer later that day.

Between the morning and evening drives, there follows a period at the camp or lodge where you are staying for those who have not taken a picnic lunch.

This is a good time to rest, clean your equipment, write postcards and read. Most safari facilities have libraries of books, usually about wildlife.

So good viewing on your Tanzanian safari or, as the Tanzanians say in Swahili, *Safari njema*, meaning have a good journey.

If you follow the above you should be basically prepared to maximize your outlay, to adapt to Africa's very special pace, and to forget the cares of your office and home.

David Martin
African Publishing Group International
Tanzania

CHECKLISTS

MAMMALS

This list includes the mammals only the visitor is most likely to see.

English	Scientific	Vernacular
PRIMATES	*PRIMATES*	
Chimpanzee	*Pan troglodytes*	*Sokwe*
Zanzibar red colobus	*Piliocolobus kirkii*	*Kima punjui*
Iringa red colobus	*Piliocolobus gordonorum*	*Mbega mwekundu*
Angola black-and-white colobus	*Colobus angolensis*	*Mbega*
Olive baboon	*Papio anubis*	*Nyani*
Yellow baboon	*Papio cynocephalus*	*Nyani*
Sanje mangabey	*Cercocebus galeritus sanjei*	*Kima*
Vervet (Savannah monkey)	*Cercopitheucus aethiops pygerythrus*	*Tumbili or Ngedere*
Sykes (Blue or Gentle) monkey	*Cercopithecus nictitans mitis*	*Kima*
Greater galago (bushbaby)	*Otolemur crassicaudatus*	*Komba*
Silver galago	*Otolemur argentata*	*Komba*
Small-eared galago	*Otolemur garnetti*	*Komba*
Senegal galago	*Galago senegalensis*	*Komba*
South African galago	*Galago moholi*	*Komba*
Spectacled galago	*Galago matschiei*	*Komba*
Rondo galago	*Galagoides rondoensis*	*Komba*
Matundu galago	*Galagoides udzungwensis*	*Komba*
Usambara galago	*Galagoides orinus*	*Komba*
Zanzibar galago	*Galagoides zanzibaricus*	*Komba*
Mozambique galago	*Galagiodes granti*	*Komba*
Thomas's galago	*Galagoides thomasi*	*Komba*

BATS   *CHIROPTERA*
This order consists of flying foxes, fruit and many other species of bats.

INSECTIVORES   *INSECTIVORA*
This order consists of otter shrews, moles, hedgehogs and shrews.

ELEPHANT SHREWS   *MACROSCELIDEA*
OR SENGIS
This order consists of soft-furred elephant shrews and giant elephant shrews.

HARES   *LAGOMORPHA*
This order consists of true hares, riverine rabbits, common rabbits, grass and rock hares.

RODENTS   *RODENTIA*
This order consists of squirrels, anomalures, spring hares, gundis, dormice, blesmols, porcupines, cane rats, dassie rats, jerboas and rat-like rodents.

CARNIVORES

CARNIVORA

Golden (Common) jackal	*Canis aureus*	*Bweha*
Side-striped jackal	*Canis adustus*	*Bweha*
Black-backed jackal	*Canis mesomelas*	*Bweha*
Bat-eared fox	*Otocyon megalotis*	*Bweha masikio*
Wild dog	*Lycaon pictus*	*Mbwa mwitu*
Zorilla	*Ictonyx striatus*	*Kicheche*
Striped weasel	*Poecilogale albinucha*	*Chororo*
Ratel (Honey badger)	*Mellivora capensis*	*Nyegere*
African clawless otter	*Aonyx capensis*	*Fisi maji mkubwa*
Spot-necked otter	*Lutra maculicollis*	*Fisi maji mdogo*
Striped hyena	*Hyaena hyaena*	*Fisi*
Spotted hyena	*Crocuta crocuta*	*Fisi*
Aardwolf	*Proteles cristata*	*Fisi ya nkole*
Common genet	*Genetta genetta*	*Kanu*
Blotched genet	*Genetta tigrina*	*Kanu*
Tree Servaline genet	*Genetta servalina*	*Kanu*
African civet	*Civettictus civetta*	*Fungo*
Wild cat	*Felis sylvestris*	*Paka pori*
Serval cat	*Felis serval*	*Mondo*
Caracal	*Felis caracal*	*Simba mangu*
Leopard	*Panthera pardus*	*Chui*
Lion	*Panthera leo*	*Simba*
Cheetah	*Acinonyx jubatus*	*Duma*

There are 23 species of mongoose and only those visitors may see are listed below:

Banded mongoose	*Mungos mungo*	*Nguchiro*
Dwarf mongoose	*Helogale parvula*	*Nguchiro*
Ichneumon mongoose	*Herpestes ichneumon*	*Nguchiro*
Slender mongoose	*Herpestes sanguinea*	*Nguchiro*
Marsh mongoose	*Atilax paludinosus*	*Nguchiro*
White-tailed mongoose	*Ichneumia albicauda*	*Nguchiro*
Bushy tailed mongoose	*Bdeogale crassicauda*	*Nguchiro*
Sokoke dog mongoose	*Bdeogale omnivora*	*Nguchiro*

SCALY ANT-EATERS

PHOLIDOTA

Tree pangolin	*Phataginus tricuspis*	*Kakakuona*
Giant pangolin	*Smutsia gigantea*	*Kakakuona*
Ground pangolin	*Smutsia temminckii*	*Kakakuona*

UNGULATES	UNGULATA	
AARDVARK	**TUBULIDENTATA**	
Aardvark	*Orycteropus afer*	*Muhanga*
HYRAXES	**HYRACOIDEA**	
Rock hyrax	*Procavia*	*Pimbi*
Bush hyrax	*Heterohyrax*	*Pimbi*
Tree hyrax	*Dendrohyrax*	*Pimbi*
PROBOSCIDS	**PROBOSCIDEA**	
African elephant	*Loxodonta africana*	*Tembo* or *Ndovu*
ODD-TOED UNGULATES	*PERISSODACTYLA*	
Burchell's zebra	*Equus burchelli*	*Punda milia*
Browse (Black) rhinoceros	*Diceros bicornis*	*Faru*
EVEN-TOED UNGULATES	*ARTIODACTYLA*	
Hippopotamus	*Hippopotamus amphibius*	*Kiboko*
Bush pig	*Potamochoerus larvatus*	*Nguruwe mwitu*
Common warthog	*Phacochoerus africanus*	*Ngiri*
Maasai giraffe	*Giraffa camelopardalis*	*Twiga*
African buffalo	*Syncerus caffer*	*Nyati* or *Mbogo*
Bushbuck	*Tragelaphus scriptus*	*Mbawala* or *Pongo*
Sitatunga	*Tragelaphus spekei*	*Nzohe*
Lesser kudu	*Tragelaphus imberbis*	*Tandala mdogo*
Greater kudu	*Tragelaphus strepsiceros*	*Tandala mkubwa*
Eland	*Taurotragus oryx*	*Pofu*
Bush duiker	*Sylvicapra grimmia*	*Nsya*
Blue duiker	*Cephalophus monticola*	*Paa*
Ader's duiker	*Cephalophus adersi*	*Paa nunga*
Natal duiker	*Cephalophus natalensis*	*Funo* or *Ngarombwi*
Harvey's duiker	*Cephalophus harveyi*	*Funo*
Suni	*Neotragus moschatus*	*Paa* or *Suni*
Sharpe's grysbok	*Raphicerus sharpei*	*Kikururu*
Steinbuck	*Raphicerus campestris*	*Dondoro* or *Isha*
Oribi	*Ourebia ourebi*	*Taya*
Klipspringer	*Oreotragus oreotragus*	*Ngurunguru* or *Mbuzi mawe*
Kirk's dikdik	*Madoqua kirkii*	*Digidigi*
Bohor reedbuck	*Redunca redunca*	*Tohe*
Southern reedbuck	*Redunca arundinum*	*Tohe ya kusini*
Puku	*Kobus vardoni*	*Puku*
Waterbuck	*Kobus ellipsiprymnus*	*Kuro*
Thomson's (red-fronted) gazelle	*Gazella rufifrons*	*Swala tomi*
Grant's gazelle	*Gazella granti*	*Swala granti*
Gerenuk	*Litocranius walleri*	*Swala twiga*
Impala	*Aepyceros melampus*	*Swala pala*
Topi	*Damaliscus lunatus*	*Nyamera*
Hartebeest	*Alcelaphus buselaphus*	*Kongoni*
Wildebeest	*Connochaetes taurinus*	*Nyumbu*
Roan antelope	*Hippotragus equinus*	*Korongo*
Sable antelope	*Hippotragus niger*	*Palahala*
Fringe-eared oryx	*Oryx beisa*	*Choroa*

BIRDS (List supplied by Liz and Neil Baker)

Ostrich
Shy Albatross
Giant Petrel
Audubon's Shearwater
Little Grebe
Great Crested Grebe
Black-necked Grebe
White-tailed Tropicbird
Cape Gannet
Masked Booby
Red-footed Booby
Brown Booby
White-breasted Cormorant
Long-tailed Cormorant
African Darter
Great White Pelican
Pink-backed Pelican
Greater Frigatebird
Lesser Frigatebird
Great Bittern
Little Bittern
Dwarf Bittern
Night Heron
White-backed Night Heron
Squacco Heron
Madagascar Squacco Heron
Rufous-bellied Heron
Cattle Egret
Green-backed Heron
Black Heron
Dimorphic Egret
Little Egret
Great White Egret
Yellow-billed Egret
Purple Heron
Grey Heron
Black-headed Heron
Goliath Heron
Hamerkop
Yellow-billed Stork
Open-billed Stork
Black Stork
Abdim's Stork
Woolly-necked Stork

White Stork
Saddle-billed Stork
Marabou Stork
Shoebill
Sacred Ibis
Glossy Ibis
Hadada Ibis
Green Ibis
African Spoonbill
Greater Flamingo
Lesser Flamingo
Fulvous Tree Duck
White-faced Tree Duck
White-backed Duck
Egyptian Goose
Spur-winged Goose
Knob-billed Duck
Pygmy Goose
Black Duck
Yellow-billed Duck
Wigeon
Cape Teal
Common Teal
Red-billed Teal
Hottentot Teal
Garganey
Cape Shoveler
Northern Shoveler
Southern Pochard
Northern Pochard
Tufted Duck
Maccoa Duck
Cuckoo Hawk
Honey Buzzard
Bat Hawk
Black-shouldered Kite
Swallow-tailed Kite
Black-billed Kite
Yellow-billed Kite
Fish Eagle
Palm-nut Vulture
Lammergeier
Egyptian Vulture
Hooded Vulture

White-backed Vulture
Rüppell's Vulture
Lappet-faced Vulture
White-headed Vulture
Black-chested Snake Eagle
Brown Snake Eagle
Southern Banded Snake Eagle
Western Banded Snake Eagle
Bateleur Eagle
Gymnogene
Eurasian Marsh Harrier
African Marsh Harrier
Pallid Harrier
Montagu's Harrier
Dark Chanting Goshawk
Pale Chanting Goshawk
Gabar Goshawk
Great Sparrowhawk
Ovambo Sparrowhawk
Levant Sparrowhawk
Eurasian Sparrowhawk
Rufous Sparrowhawk
Little Sparrowhawk
African Goshawk
Shikra
Grasshopper Buzzard
Lizard Buzzard
Steppe Buzzard
Mountain Buzzard
Long-legged Buzzard
Augur Buzzard
Wahlberg's Eagle
Greater Spotted Eagle
Lesser Spotted Eagle
Tawny Eagle
Steppe Eagle
Imperial Eagle
Verreaux's Eagle
African Hawk Eagle
Booted Eagle
Ayres' Hawk Eagle
Long-crested Eagle
Crowned Eagle
Martial Eagle

Osprey
Secretary Bird
Lesser Kestrel
Common Kestrel
Rock Kestrel
White-eyed Kestrel
Grey Kestrel
Dickinson's Kestrel
Pygmy Falcon
Red-footed Falcon
Amur Falcon
Red-necked Falcon
Eleonora's Falcon
Lanner Falcon
Saker Falcon
Taita Falcon
Barbary Falcon
Peregrine Falcon
Eurasian Hobby
African Hobby
Coqui Francolin
Forest Francolin
Crested Francolin
Ring-necked Francolin
Shelley's Francolin
Red-winged Francolin
Hildebrandt's Francolin
Scaly Francolin
Red-necked Spurfowl
Grey-breasted Spurfowl
Yellow-necked Spurfowl
Udzungwa Forest Partridge
Common Quail
Harlequin Quail
Blue Quail
Crested Guineafowl
Kenya Crested Guineafowl
Vulturine Guineafowl
Helmeted Guineafowl
Common Buttonquail
Black-rumped Buttonquail
White-spotted Flufftail
Buff-spotted Flufftail
Red-chested Flufftail
Long-toed Flufftail
Streaky-breasted Flufftail
Striped Flufftail

African Water Rail
Corncrake
African Crake
Black Crake
Baillon's Crake
Spotted Crake
Striped Crake
Purple Gallinule
Allen's Gallinule
Lesser Moorhen
Common Moorhen
Red-knobbed Coot
Wattled Crane
Grey Crowned Crane
African Finfoot
Denham's Bustard
Kori Bustard
Buff-crested Bustard
White-bellied Bustard
Hartlaub's Bustard
Jacana
Lesser Jacana
Painted Snipe
Oystercatcher
Black-winged Stilt
Avocet
Crab Plover
Eurasian Stone Curlew
Water Thicknee
Spotted Thicknee
Two-banded Courser
Heuglin's Courser
Violet-tipped Courser
Temminck's Courser
Collared Pratincole
Black-winged Pratincole
Madagascar Pratincole
Rock Pratincole
Quail-plover
Little Ringed Plover
Ringed Plover
Kittlitz's Plover
Three-banded Plover
Forbes' Plover
White-fronted Plover
Chestnut-banded Plover
Lesser Sandplover

Greater Sandplover
Caspian Plover
Pacific Golden Plover
Grey Plover
Wattled Plover
White-crowned Plover
Black-headed Plover
Blacksmith Plover
Spur-winged Plover
Brown-chested Plover
Senegal Plover
Black-winged Plover
Crowned Plover
Long-toed Plover
Common Snipe
African Snipe
Great Snipe
Jack Snipe
Black-tailed Godwit
Bar-tailed Godwit
Whimbrel
Curlew
Spotted Redshank
Redshank
Greenshank
Marsh Sandpiper
Green Sandpiper
Wood Sandpiper
Terek Sandpiper
Common Sandpiper
Ruddy Turnstone
Red Knot
Sanderling
Little Stint
Temminck's Stint
Long-toed Stint
Curlew Sandpiper
Broad-billed Sandpiper
Ruff
Red-necked Phalarope
Pomarine Skua
Long-tailed Skua
Arctic Skua
Sooty Gull
Kelp Gull
Lesser Black-backed Gull
Heuglin's Gull

Black-headed Gull
Grey-headed Gull
Gull-billed Tern
Caspian Tern
Swift Tern
Lesser Crested Tern
Sandwich Tern
Black-naped Tern
Roseate Tern
Common Tern
White-cheeked Tern
Bridled Tern
Sooty Tern
Little Tern
Saunder's Tern
Whiskered Tern
White-winged Tern
Brown Noddy
African Skimmer
Chestnut-bellied Sandgrouse
Black-faced Sandgrouse
Yellow-throated Sandgrouse
Speckled Pigeon
Afep Pigeon
Olive Pigeon
Eastern Bronze-naped Pigeon
Lemon Dove
Turtle Dove
Dusky Turtle Dove
Laughing Dove
Mourning Dove
Ring-necked Dove
Red-eyed Dove
Emerald-spotted Wood Dove
Blue-spotted Wood Dove
Tambourine Dove
Namaqua Dove
Pemba Green Pigeon
African Green Pigeon
Grey Parrot
Brown-necked Parrot
Red-fronted Parrot
Orange-bellied Parrot
Brown Parrot
Brown-headed Parrot
Red-headed Lovebird
Fischer's Lovebird

Yellow-collared Lovebird
Lilian's Lovebird
Black-billed Turaco
Livingstone's Turaco
Schalow's Turaco
Fischer's Turaco
Hartlaub's Turaco
Purple-crested Turaco
Ross's Turaco
Great Blue Turaco
Eastern Grey Plantain Eater
Grey Go-away Bird
Bare-faced Go-away Bird
White-bellied Go-away Bird
Great Spotted Cuckoo
Jacobin Cuckoo
Levaillant's Cuckoo
Thick-billed Cuckoo
Red-chested Cuckoo
Black Cuckoo
Common Cuckoo
African Cuckoo
Asian Lesser Cuckoo
Madagascar Cuckoo
Dusky Long-tailed Cuckoo
Barred Long-tailed Cuckoo
Emerald Cuckoo
Klaas' Cuckoo
Didric Cuckoo
Yellowbill
Black Coucal
Blue-headed Coucal
Coppery-tailed Coucal
Senegal Coucal
White-browed Coucal
Burchell's Coucal
Barn Owl
Grass Owl
Sokoke Scops Owl
Eurasian Scops Owl
African Scops Owl
Pemba Scops Owl
White-faced Owl
Cape Eagle Owl
Spotted Eagle Owl
Usambara Eagle Owl
Verreaux's Eagle Owl

Pel's Fishing Owl
Pearl-spotted Owlet
Barred Owlet
African Wood Owl
Short-eared Owl
African Marsh Owl
Eurasian Nightjar
Rufous-cheeked Nightjar
Fiery-necked Nightjar
Dusky Nightjar
Donaldson-Smith's Nightjar
Montane Nightjar
Usambara Nightjar
Ruwenzori Nightjar
Swamp Nightjar
Plain Nightjar
Freckled Nightjar
Gabon Nightjar
Slender-tailed Nightjar
Standard-winged Nightjar
Pennant-winged Nightjar
Scarce Swift
Mottled Spinetail
Böhm's Spinetail
Palm Swift
Alpine Swift
Mottled Swift
Nyanza Swift
Forbes-Watson's Swift
Eurasian Swift
Black Swift
Little Swift
Horus Swift
White-rumped Swift
Speckled Mousebird
White-headed Mousebird
Blue-naped Mousebird
Red-faced Mousebird
Narina Trogon
Bar-tailed Trogon
Malachite Kingfisher
Half-collared Kingfisher
White-bellied Kingfisher
Shining Blue Kingfisher
Pygmy Kingfisher
Brown-hooded Kingfisher
Chestnut-bellied Kingfisher

Blue-breasted Kingfisher
Woodland Kingfisher
Mangrove Kingfisher
Striped Kingfisher
Giant Kingfisher
Pied Kingfisher
Little Bee-eater
Blue-breasted Bee-eater
Cinnamon Bee-eater
Swallow-tailed Bee-eater
White-fronted Bee-eater
Somali Bee-eater
White-throated Bee-eater
Böhm's Bee-eater
Madagascar Bee-eater
Blue-cheeked Bee-eater
Eurasian Bee-eater
Northern Carmine Bee-eater
Southern Carmine Bee-eater
Eurasian Roller
Lilac-breasted Roller
Racket-tailed Roller
Rufous-crowned Roller
Broad-billed Roller
Green Wood Hoopoe
Violet Wood Hoopoe
White-headedWood Hoopoe
Forest Wood Hoopoe
Common Scimitarbill
Abyssinian Scimitarbill
African Hoopoe
Eurasian Hoopoe
Red-billed Hornbill
Ruaha Hornbill
Yellow-billed Hornbill
Von der Decken's Hornbill
Pied Hornbill
Crowned Hornbill
Pale-billed Hornbill
Grey Hornbill
Trumpeter Hornbill
Black & White Casqued Hornbill
Silvery-cheeked Hornbill
Southern Ground Hornbill
Grey-throated Barbet
White-eared Barbet
Whyte's Barbet

Green Barbet
Yellow-spotted Barbet
Green Tinkerbird
Moustached Green Tinkerbird
Red-fronted Tinkerbird
Yellow-fronted Tinkerbird
Yellow-rumped Tinkerbird
Spot-flanked Barbet
Red-fronted Barbet
Miombo Pied Barbet
Black-throated Barbet
Hairy-breasted Barbet
Black-collared Barbet
Black-billed Barbet
Red-faced Barbet
Brown-breasted Barbet
White-headed Barbet
Black-backed Barbet
Double-toothed Barbet
Crested Barbet
Red and Yellow Barbet
d'Arnaud's Barbet
Usambiro Barbet
Eastern Honeybird
Wahlberg's Honeybird
Scaly-throated Honeyguide
Greater Honeyguide
Lesser Honeyguide
Least Honeyguide
Pallid Honeyguide
Red-throated Wryneck
Nubian Woodpecker
Bennett's Woodpecker
Speckle-throated Woodpecker
Golden-tailed Woodpecker
Mombasa Woodpecker
Little Spotted Woodpecker
Fine-banded Woodpecker
Buff-spotted Woodpecker
Brown-eared Woodpecker
Cardinal Woodpecker
Stierling's Woodpecker
Grey Woodpecker
Grey-headed Woodpecker
Olive Woodpecker
Bearded Woodpecker
Yellow-crested Woodpecker

Brown-backed Woodpecker
African Broadbill
African pitta
Singing Bush Lark
White-tailed Lark
Friedmann's Lark
Rufous-naped Lark
Red-winged Bush Lark
Angola Lark
Flappet Lark
Fawn-coloured Lark
Pink-breasted Lark
Dusky Bush Lark
Beesley's Lark
Red-capped Lark
Athi Short-toed Lark
Short-tailed Lark
Chestnut-backed Sparrowlark
Fischer's Sparrowlark
Black Roughwing
Eastern Roughwing
White-headed Roughwing
Mascarene Martin
Sand Martin
African Sand Martin
Banded Martin
Grey-rumped Swallow
Rufous-chested Swallow
Mosque Swallow
Lesser Striped Swallow
Greater Striped Swallow
Red-rumped Swallow
African Rock Martin
Blue Swallow
Wire-tailed Swallow
Pearl-breasted Swallow
Ethiopian Swallow
White-throated Swallow
European Swallow
Angola Swallow
House Martin
Yellow Wagtail
Cape Wagtail
Grey Wagtail
Mountain Wagtail
White Wagtail
African Pied Wagtail

Golden Pipit
African Pipit
Jackson's Pipit
Long-billed Pipit
Woodland Pipit
Plain-backed Pipit
Buffy Pipit
Short-tailed Pipit
Bush Pipit
Tree Pipit
Sokoke Pipit
Red-throated Pipit
Striped Pipit
Yellow-throated Longclaw
Fülleborn's Longclaw
Pangani Longclaw
Rosy-breasted Longclaw
Black Cuckoo Shrike
Purple-throated Cuckoo Shrike
Grey Cuckoo Shrike
White-breasted Cuckoo Shrike
Shelley's Greenbul
Mountain Greenbul
Green-throated Greenbul
"Uluguru" Greenbul
"Poroto" Greenbul
Stripe-cheeked Greenbul
Little Greenbul
Cameroon Sombre Greenbul
Slender-billed Greenbul
Little Grey Greenbul
Yellow-whiskered Greenbul
Zanzibar Sombre Greenbul
Honeyguide Greenbul
Joyful Greenbul
Yellow-throated Leaflove
Yellow-bellied Greenbul
Leaflove
Terrestrial Brownbul
Northern Brownbul
Toro Olive Greenbul
Grey-olive Greenbul
Fischer's Greenbul
Cabanis' Greenbul
Olive Mountain Greenbul
Icterine Greenbul
Xavier's Greenbul

Yellow-streaked Greenbul
Sharpe's Greenbul
Tiny Greenbul
Red-tailed Bristlebill
Yellow-lored Bristlebill
Spotted Greenbul
Yellow-vented Bulbul
White-tailed Ant-thrush
Red-tailed Ant-thrush
Rufous Thrush
Rock Thrush
Little Rock Thrush
Miombo Rock Thrush
Olive Thrush
African Thrush
Kurrichane Thrush
Bare-eyed Thrush
Groundscraper Thrush
Spotted Ground Thrush
Orange Ground Thrush
Abyssinian Ground Thrush
Fire-crested Alethe
Brown-chested Alethe
White-chested Alethe
Starred Robin
Forest Robin
Swynnerton's Robin
Bocage's Akalat
Alexander's Akalat
Lowland Akalat
Sharpe's Akalat
East Coast Akalat
Usambara Akalat
Iringa Akalat
"Rubeho" Akalat
Sprosser
Nightingale
Irania
Olive-flanked Robin Chat
Grey-winged Robin Chat
Cape Robin Chat
Blue-shouldered Robin Chat
Rüppell's Robin Chat
White-browed Robin Chat
Red-capped Robin Chat
Snowy-crowned Robin Chat
Collared Palm Thrush

Spotted Morning Thrush
Miombo Scrub Robin
Bearded Scrub Robin
Brown-backed Scrub Robin
White-browed Scrub Robin
Rufous Bush Chat
Redstart
Stonechat
Whinchat
Northern Wheatear
Pied Wheatear
Schalow's Wheatear
Capped Wheatear
Isabelline Wheatear
Familiar Chat
Alpine Chat
Northern Anteater Chat
Sooty Chat
White-headed Black Chat
Cliff Chat
Broad-tailed Warbler
Little Rush Warbler
White-winged Warbler
Cinnamon Bracken Warbler
Evergreen Forest Warbler
Bamboo Warbler
Black-faced Rufous Warbler
Mrs Moreau's Warbler
African Moustached Warbler
River Warbler
Sedge Warbler
African Reed Warbler
Reed Warbler
Marsh Warbler
Great Reed Warbler
Basra Reed Warbler
Lesser Swamp Warbler
Greater Swamp Warbler
Olivaceous Warbler
Upcher's Warbler
Olive-tree Warbler
Icterine Warbler
Papyrus Yellow Warbler
Yellow Warbler
Mountain Yellow Warbler
Green-capped Eremomela
Black-collared Eremomela

Yellow-bellied Eremomela
Yellow-vented Eremomela
White-browed Crombec
Green Crombec
Red-capped Crombec
Red-faced Crombec
Long-billed Crombec
Northern Crombec
Somali Long-billed Crombec
Grey Longbill
Yellow Longbill
Kretschmer's Longbill
Willow Warbler
Chiffchaff
Wood Warbler
Brown Forest Warbler
Yellow-throated Warbler
Laura's Warbler
Yellow-bellied Hyliota
Usambara Hyliota
Green Hylia
Barred Warbler
Garden Warbler
Blackcap
Common Whitethroat
Banded Parisoma
Brown Parisoma
Pectoral-patch Cisticola
Pale-crowned Cisticola
Wing-snapping Cisticola
Black-backed Cisticola
Zitting Cisticola
Desert Cisticola
Croaking Cisticola
Stout Cisticola
Wailing Cisticola
Ashy Cisticola
Rattling Cisticola
Churring Cisticola
Tiny Cisticola
Siffling Cisticola
Tabora Cisticola
Piping Cisticola
Rock-loving Cisticola
Lazy Cisticola
Trilling Cisticola
Red-faced Cisticola

Singing Cisticola
Hunter's Cisticola
Kilombero Cisticola
Chubb's Cisticola
Black-lored Cisticola
Winding Cisticola
White-tailed Cisticola
Carruthers' Cisticola
Chirping Cisticola
Levaillant's Cisticola
Tawny-flanked Prinia
White-chinned Prinia
Red-winged Warbler
Red-fronted Warbler
Buff-bellied Warbler
Yellow-breasted Apalis
Masked Apalis
Black-throated Apalis
White-winged Apalis
Bar-throated Apalis
Grey Apalis
Brown-headed Apalis
Karamoja Apalis
Buff-throated Apalis
Kungwe Apalis
Chestnut-throated Apalis
Chapin's Apalis
Black-headed Apalis
Long-billed Tailorbird
Red-capped Tailorbird
Grey-backed Camaroptera
Green-backed Camaroptera
Olive-green Camaroptera
Pale Wren Warbler
Barred Wren Warbler
Grey Wren Warbler
Grey-capped Warbler
Grey Flycatcher
Pale Flycatcher
Silverbird
White-eyed Slaty Flycatcher
Southern Black Flycatcher
Western Black Flycatcher
Collared Flycatcher
Semi-collared Flycatcher
Spotted Flycatcher
Dusky Flycatcher

Swamp Flycatcher
Ashy Flycatcher
Sooty Flycatcher
Böhm's Flycatcher
Lead-coloured Flycatcher
Grey-throated Flycatcher
Vanga Flycatcher
Shrike Flycatcher
Forest Batis
Reichenow's Batis
Chin-spot Batis
East Coast Batis
Pygmy Batis
Black-headed Batis
Yellow-bellied Wattle-eye
Jameson's Wattle-eye
Chestnut Wattle-eye
Brown-throated Wattle-eye
Black-throated Wattle-eye
Livingstone's Flycatcher
Little Yellow Flycatcher
Blue Flycatcher
White-tailed Blue Flycatcher
Dusky Crested Flycatcher
White-tailed Crested Flycatcher
Crested Flycatcher
Paradise Flycatcher
Red-bellied Paradise Flycatcher
Spot-throat
Dappled Mountain Robin
Brown Illadopsis
Mountain Illadopsis
Pale-breasted Illadopsis
Scaly-breasted Illadopsis
African Hill Babbler
Arrow-marked Babbler
Brown Babbler
Black-lored Babbler
Northern Pied Babbler
Angola Babbler
Rufous Chatterer
Scaly Chatterer
Acacia Grey Tit
Miombo Grey Tit
Black Tit
White-shouldered Black Tit
White-bellied Tit

Red-throated Tit
Cinnamon-breasted Tit
Mouse-coloured Penduline Tit
African Penduline Tit
Buff-bellied Penduline Tit
Spotted Creeper
Grey-headed Sunbird
Plain-backed Sunbird
Anchieta's Sunbird
Western Violet-backed Sunbird
Eastern Violet-backed Sunbird
Uluguru Violet-backed Sunbird
Amani Sunbird
Green Sunbird
Banded Green Sunbird
Collared Sunbird
Little Green Sunbird
Eastern Olive Sunbird
Western Olive Sunbird
Mouse-coloured Sunbird
Green-headed Sunbird
Blue-throated Sunbird
Green-throated Sunbird
Amethyst Sunbird
Scarlet-chested Sunbird
Hunter's Sunbird
Variable Sunbird
White-bellied Sunbird
Oustalet's Sunbird
Rufous-winged Sunbird
Olive-bellied Sunbird
Miombo Sunbird
Eastern Double-collared Sunbird
"fülleborn's" Sunbird
"rubeho" sunbird
Moreau's Sunbird
Loveridge's Sunbird
Regal Sunbird
Shelley's Sunbird
Mariqua Sunbird
Orange-tufted Sunbird
Red-chested Sunbird
Black-bellied Sunbird
Purple-banded Sunbird
Tsavo Sunbird
Pemba Sunbird

Copper Sunbird
Tacazze Sunbird
Beautiful Sunbird
Malachite Sunbird
Scarlet-tufted Sunbird
Superb Sunbird
Bronze Sunbird
Golden-winged Sunbird
Abyssinian White-eye
Montane White-eye
South Pare White-eye
Yellow White-eye
Pemba White-eye
Golden Oriole
African Golden Oriole
Black-headed Oriole
Montane Oriole
Green-headed Oriole
Western Black-headed Oriole
Souza's Shrike
Red-backed Shrike
Red-tailed Shrike
Mackinnon's Shrike
Lesser Grey Shrike
Grey-backed Fiscal
Long-tailed Fiscal
Taita Fiscal
Common Fiscal
Woodchat Shrike
Masked Shrike
Uhehe Fiscal
Magpie Shrike
White-capped Shrike
Brubru
Pringle's Puffback
Black-backed Puffback
Northern Puffback
Pink-footed Puffback
Marsh Tchagra
Anchieta's Tchagra
Brown-crowned Tchagra
Three-streaked Tchagra
Black-crowned Tchagra
Rosy-patched Shrike
Lühder's Bush Shrike
Tropical Boubou

Black-headed Gonolek
Papyrus Gonolek
Fülleborn's Boubou
Slate-coloured Boubou
Sulphur-breasted Bush Shrike
Black-fronted Bush Shrike
Four-coloured Bush Shrike
Grey-headed Bush Shrike
Uluguru Bush Shrike
Western Nicator
Eastern Nicator
White Helmet Shrike
Grey-crested Helmet Shrike
Retz's Helmet Shrike
Chestnut-fronted Helmet Shrike
Square-tailed Drongo
Drongo
Indian House Crow
Pied Crow
Cape Rook
White-necked Raven
Stuhlmann's Starling
Kenrick's Starling
Waller's Starling
Red-winged Starling
Chestnut-winged Starling
Slender-billed Starling
Black-breasted Starling
Blue-eared Starling
Lesser Blue-eared Starling
Sharp-tailed Starling
Splendid Starling
Rüppell's Starling
Superb Starling
Shelley's Starling
Hildebrandt's Starling
Fischer's Starling
Golden-breasted Starling
Ashy Starling
Abbott's Starling
Sharpe's Starling
Violet-backed Starling
Magpie Starling
White-winged Starling
Wattled Starling
Yellow-billed Oxpecker

Red-billed Oxpecker
House Sparrow
Rufous Sparrow
Grey-headed Sparrow
Swahili Sparrow
Parrot-billed Sparrow
Southern Grey-headed Sparrow
Chestnut Sparrow
Java Sparrow
Yellow-spotted Petronia
White-browed Petronia
Red-billed Buffalo Weaver
White-headed Buffalo Weaver
Speckle-fronted Weaver
White-browed Sparrow Weaver
Chestnut-mantled Sparrow Weaver
Rufous-tailed Weaver
Grey-headed Social Weaver
Black-capped Social Weaver
Baglafecht Weaver
Bertram's Weaver
Slender-billed Weaver
Little Weaver
Black-necked Weaver
Spectacled Weaver
Black-billed Weaver
Golden Weaver
Holub's Golden Weaver
Orange Weaver
Golden Palm Weaver
Taveta Golden Weaver
Southern Brown-throated Weaver
Northern Brown-throated Weaver
Kilombero Weaver
Masked Weaver
Vitelline Masked Weaver
Tanganyika Masked Weaver
Speke's Weaver
Vieillot's Black Weaver
Village Weaver
Weyns' Weaver
Yellow-backed Weaver
Golden-backed Weaver
Chestnut Weaver
Dark-backed Weaver
Brown-capped Weaver
Olive-headed Weaver

Usambara Weaver
Compact Weaver
Parasitic Weaver
Grosbeak Weaver
Red-headed Weaver
Red-headed Malimbe
Cardinal Quelea
Red-headed Quelea
Red-billed Quelea
Yellow-crowned Bishop
Fire-fronted Bishop
Black Bishop
Black-winged Red Bishop
Zanzibar Red Bishop
Southern Red Bishop
Yellow Bishop
Fan-tailed Widowbird
Yellow-mantled Widowbird
White-winged Widowbird
Red-collared Widowbird
Marsh Widowbird
Mountain Marsh Widowbird
Jackson's Widowbird
Jameson's Antpecker
Grey-headed Negrofinch
White-breasted Negrofinch
White-collared Oliveback
Green-winged Pytilia
Orange-winged Pytilia
Red-faced Crimsonwing
Abyssinian Crimsonwing
Black-bellied Seedcracker
Lesser Seedcracker
Red-headed Bluebill
Peters' Twinspot
Green-backed Twinspot
Brown Firefinch
Red-billed Firefinch
African Firefinch
Jameson's Firefinch
Black-tailed Waxbill
Yellow-bellied Waxbill
Fawn-breasted Waxbill
Crimson-rumped Waxbill
Black-rumped Waxbill
Common Waxbill
Black-crowned Waxbill

Black-faced Waxbill
Southern Cordonbleu
Red-cheeked Cordonbleu
Blue-capped Cordonbleu
Purple Grenadier
Zebra Waxbill
Oriole Finch
Locust Finch
Quailfinch
Black-chinned Quailfinch
Common Silverbill
Grey-headed Silverbill
Bronze Mannikin
Black-and-White Mannikin
Rufous-backed Mannikin
Magpie Mannikin
Cut-throat
Village Indigobird
Dusky Indigobird
Twinspot Indigobird
Purple Indigobird
Pin-tailed Whydah
Steel-blue Whydah
Straw-tailed Whydah
Eastern Paradise Whydah
Broad-tailed Whydah
Western Citril
East African Citril
Yellow-crowned Canary
Papyrus Canary
Black-throated Canary
Yellow-rumped Seedeater
Yellow-fronted Canary
White-bellied Canary
Southern Grosbeak Canary
Brimstone Canary
Black-eared Seedeater
Stripe-breasted Seedeater
Streaky Seedeater
Yellow-browed Seedeater
Thick-billed Seedeater
Kipengere Seedeater
Cinnamon Rock Bunting
Southern Rock Bunting
Somali Bunting
Golden-breasted Bunting
Cabanis' Bunting

FURTHER READING

Kingdon, Jonathan, *African Mammals*, Academic Press, 1997

Skinner, J.D. & Smithers, R.H.N., *The Mammals of the Southern African Sub-region*, University of Pretoria, 1990

Zimmerman, Dale et al, *Birds of Kenya and Northern Tanzania*, Christopher Helm, 1996

Kielland, Jan, *Butterflies of Tanzania*, Hill House, 1990

Congdon, Colin & Collins, Steve, *Supplement to Butterflies of Tanzania*, Lambillionea, 1998

Beentje, Henk, *Kenya Trees, Shrubs and Lianas*, National Museum of Kenya, 1994

Moffet J.P. (ed), *Handbook of Tanganyika*, Government of Tanganyika, 1958

Smith, Anthony, *The Great Rift: Africa's Changing Valley*, BBC Books, 1998

Keller, Peter C., *Gemstones of East Africa*, Geoscience Press Inc, 1992

Spear, Thomas, *Mountain Farmers*, James Currey, 1997

Bigger, M., *Some Wild Flowers of Kilimanjaro*, Kilimanjaro Mountain Club, 1966

Hemingway, Ernest, *The Snows of Kilimanjaro*, Charles Scribner's Sons, 1927

Reader, John, *Kilimanjaro*, Elm Tree Books, 1982

Schneppen, Heinz, *Why Kilimanjaro is in Tanzania*, National Museums of Tanzania

Stahl, Kathleen, *Outline of Chagga History*, Tanganyika Notes and Records, 1965

Douglas-Hamilton, I & O, *Among the Elephants*, Penguin, 1968

Arhem, Kaj, *Pastoral Man in the Garden of Eden*, Uppsala, 1985

Thompson, D.M. (ed), *Multiple Land Use: The Experience of Ngorongoro*, IUCN, 1997

Fosbrooke, Henry, *Ngorongoro: The Eighth Wonder*, Andre Deutsch,

Saitoti, Tepilit Ole & Beckwith Carol, *Maasai*, Harvill, 1980

Leakey, Mary, *Olduvai Gorge: My Search for Early Man*, Collins, 1979

Darwin, Charles, *The Origin of Species*, Penguin, 1968

Sinclair, A.R.E. & Arcese, Peter (eds), *Serengeti 11*, University of Chicago, 1995

Lawick, Hugo van, *Savage Paradise*, Collins, 1997

Schaller, George, *Golden Shadows, Flying Hooves*, Collins, 1974

Grzimek, Bernard & Michael, *Serengeti Shall Not Die*, Hamish Hamilton, 1960

Mmari, C.J.B., *The Lake Manyara-Tarangire-Simanjoro Complex*, University of Norway, 1989

Richmond, Matthew (ed), *The Seashores of Eastern Africa*, SIDA, 1997

Hall, Richard, *Empires of the Monsoon: A History of the Indian Ocean and its Invaders*, Harper Collins, 1996

Davidson, Basil, *The Lost Cities of Africa*, Little Brown, 1987

Lovejoy, Paul, *Transformations in Slavery: A History of Slavery in Africa*, CUP, 1983

Reader, John, *Africa: A Biography of the Continent*, Hamish Hamilton, 1997

Sherrif, Abdul, *Slaves, Spices and Ivory in Zanzibar*, James Currey, 1987

Alpers, Edward, *The East African Slave Trade*, East African Publishing House, 1967

Whitely, W.H., *Tippu Tip*, East African Literature Bureau, 1959

Sherrif, Abdul & Ferguson Ed (eds), *Zanzibar Under Colonial Rule*, James Currey, 1991

Reute, Emily, *Memoirs of an Arabian Princess from Zanzibar*, Markus Weiner, 1996

Lofchie, Michael, *Zanzibar: Background to Revolution*, Princeton University Press, 1968

Patience, Kevin, *The Shortest War*, (Self-published), 1994

Patience, Kevin, *The Loss of H.M.S. Pegasus*, (Self-published), 1995

Rau, Uwe, *Doors in Zanzibar*, Goethe Institute, Dar es Salaam, 1995

Sherrif, Abdul, *The History & Conservation of Zanzibar Stone Town*, Department of Archives, Museums and Antiquities, Zanzibar, 1995

Else, David, *Guide to Zanzibar*, Bradt Publications, 1995

Lovett, Jon & Wasser, Samuel, *Biogeography and Ecology of the Rain Forests of Eastern Africa*, CUP, 1993

Burgess, N.D., et al, *Biodiversity of Conservation of the Eastern Arc Mountains of Kenya and Tanzania*, Morogoro, Tanzania, 1997

Kingdon, Jonathan, *Island Africa: The Evolution of Africa's Rare Animals and Plants*, Collins, 1990
Mbuya, L.H. et al, *Useful Trees and Shrubs for Tanzania*, Sida, 1994
Ehardt, Carolyn & Struhsaker, Thomas, *Conservation of Endangered Endemic Primates of the Udzungwa Mountains*, funding proposal, 1999
Hoyle, David, *Udzungwa Mountains National Park: Socio-Economic Survey*, TANAPA/WWF, 1997
Lovett, John, *The Eastern Arc Forests of Tanzania*, Kew magazine, 1986
Rodgers, W.A, & Homewood, K.M., *Biological Values and Conservation Prospects for the Forest and Primate Populations of the Udzungwa Mountains*, Applied Science Publishers, 1982
Cory, H., *The People of the Lake Victoria Region*, Tanganyika Notes and Records, 1952
Moorehead, Alan, *The White Nile*, Penguin Books, 1973
Moorehead, Alan, *The Blue Nile*, Penguin Books, 1983
Mallory, Kenneth, et al, *Lake Victoria: Africa's Inland Sea*, New England Aquarium, 1999
Ross, Charles, (ed), *Crocodiles and Alligators*, Merehurst Press, 1990
Price Waterhouse/Ian Games, *Preliminary Tourism Plan for the Northern Sector of the Selous Game Reserve*- Vol 1 Background, 1997
Robins, Eric, *Secret Eden: Africa's Enchanted Wilderness*, Elm Tree Books, 1980
Millais. J.G., *Life of Frederick Courtenay Selous*, Gallery Publications, 2001
Itani, Dr Junichiro, *Mahale*, Japanese International Cooperation Agency, 1980
Games, Ian, *Katavi-Rukwa Ecosystem*, TANAPA, 2002
Davenport, Dr Tim, & Ndangalasi, Dr Henry, *The Orchids of Kitulo Plateau*, Oryx, CUP, 2003

AFRICAN PUBLISHING GROUP
Into Africa Travel Guides on Tanzania *(* denotes forthcoming)*

by David Martin

Tanzania

Serengeti: Endless Plains
Ngorongoro: Book of Life
Kilimanjaro: Africa's Beacon
Zanzibar: Spice Islands
Udzungwa Mountains National Park
Ruaha National Park
Mikumi National Park
Lake Manyara National Park
Arusha Town, Park and Mount Meru
Lake Victoria including Rubondo Island
Saadani and Bagamoyo
Tarangire National Park
Olduvai and Laetoli
Mafia Marine Park and Kilwa
Selous Game Reserve
Tanzania National Parks and Other Attractions

Birds of Tanzania (checklist)
*Gombe National Park and Kigoma**
*Mahale National Park and Lake Tanganyika**
*Katavi National Park**
*Kitulo Plateau**
*Dar es Salaam**
*Mnazi Bay Marine Park**
*Mammals of Tanzania**
Mammals of Tanzania (checklist)*
*Birds of Tanzania**
*Insects of Tanzania**
*Trees of Tanzania**
*Reptiles and Amphibians of Tanzania**
*Gemstones of Tanzania**
*Tanzania National Guide**
*Tanzania in Pictures**

INDEX